WHAT OTHERS SAY ABOUT MICHAEL SAMUELSON AND HIS WORK

Michael…You are among a very select group of distinguished leaders, scientists, activists, and public figures.

—George H.W. Bush, former President of the United States

Thank you for helping our stakeholders turn on their radar.

—Willie G. Davidson, Harley-Davidson Motor Company

Through life's journey you have successfully captured stories [*Voices from the Edge*] of extraordinary individuals who have found peace and happiness to succeed. I applaud your dedication.

—Tom Ridge, former Secretary, US Office of Homeland Security

You also have the knack of maintaining what I know you strive for, and this is a coterie of individuals diverse, yet with one overriding common concern [*Voices from the Edge*]. You have done it well.

—C. Everett Koop, MD, ScD, former US Surgeon General

Your presentation was truly inspiring and made a significant contribution to the resounding success of the summit [Steps to a Healthier US—Keynote Address].

—Richard H. Carmona, MD, former US Surgeon General

What a marvelous inspirational book [*Voices from the Edge*] you have put together—it is so touching as one reads each story. However, I am not surprised after meeting you and hearing you speak.

—Mrs. Betty Ford, former US First Lady

This is a compelling book [*Voices from the Edge*] that moves your heart. Read it and share it with others.

—Ken H. Blanchard, coauthor of *The One Minute Manager* and *Gung Ho!*

A really powerful and very important book [*Voices from the Edge*] with life lessons for everyone. Five stars!

—Larry King, *Larry King Live*, CNN

Engaging, enlightening, challenging, and inspiring! [*What Would Mickey Say: Coaching Men to Health and Happiness*] The Coach gives tips that can change our lives.

—James O. Prochaska, PhD, author of *Changing for Good*

Long known in the cancer community for his dedication and passion, Michael Samuelson extends his mission in these pages. We encourage you to read this book, *What Would Mickey Say: Coaching Men to Health and Happiness*, and share it with others.

—The Livestrong Foundation

BEYOND
CANCER
SURVIVAL

Living a Life of Thrival

BEYOND
CANCER
SURVIVAL

Living a Life of Thrival

MICHAEL SAMUELSON

GREEN GLASS
PUBLISHING

CANTON, MICHIGAN

Permission to reproduce or transmit in any form or by any means, electronic, or mechanical, including photocopying and recording, or by an information storage and retrieval system, must be obtained by writing to the author at the following address:

Green Glass Publishing
Logan S. Moore, Publisher
2363 Lexington Circle North
Canton, MI 48188
m.samuelson@mac.com
www.SamuelsonWellness.com

Editing: Write On, Inc.
Text Design/Production: Concierge Marketing, Inc. Publishing Services
Cover Photo: Michael Samuelson, taken in the Himalayas in Nepal by Gary Ruff

Paperback ISBN: 978-0-9710216-5-5
Kindle ISBN: 978-0-9710216-6-2
EPUB ISBN: 978-0-9710216-7-9

Library of Congress Control Number: 2015936485
Library of Congress Cataloging Information on file with the publisher.

Disclaimer: The information contained in these topics is not intended nor implied to be a substitute for professional medical advice. It is provided for educational purposes only. You assume full responsibility for how you choose to use this information. Always seek the advice of your physician or other qualified healthcare provider before starting any new treatment or discontinuing an existing treatment. Talk with your healthcare provider about any questions you may have regarding a medical condition. This information should not be used as a substitute for the care and knowledge that your physician can provide.

10 9 8 7 6 5 4 3 2 1

*To All Cancer Survivors and Thrivers
Yesterday, Today, and Tomorrow*

CLOSE THE DOOR WHEN YOU LEAVE

An Open Notice to Cancer

Written for the dedication of the University of Michigan Comprehensive Cancer Center for Healing Arts

—Michael Hayes Samuelson

I never asked you to visit…at least I don't believe I did
Maybe…I don't know
It's so confusing

At any rate, you're a rude guest
You take my energy, rob my sleep, and with a stick
You swirl and distort my dreams

All right, you are here—for now
But understand
There are two places that are forever off limits

You may not tread on my spirit
You may not occupy my soul

I have heard of your visits to others
I know the damage you leave in your path
The wanton disregard for innocence, value,
and what some would call fairness

Also, I hear that laughter confuses you;
that good foods make you feel bad, and
That nothing causes you more distress than an
autumn sunset, the forever blue of a summer sky,
Or the unconditional radiance of a child's smile

Listen and understand
You might pilfer my closets, empty all the drawers,
and trash my house
But there are two places forever off limits

You may not tread on my spirit
You may not occupy my soul

Do not mistake my nausea, weakness,
and pain as signs of your victory
They are simply small dents in the armor I wear to fight you
Instead, look deeply into my eyes

They will once again remind you that there
are two places forever off limits

You must not…
May not…
Will not tread on my spirit

You must not…
May not…
Will not occupy my soul

CONTENTS

PREFACE

OF THE MILLIONS OF BOOKS PUBLISHED EACH YEAR, WHY DID you pick up this book? And why should you continue reading?

Well, the answer to the first question is relatively easy. You either

- Liked the cover

- Were intrigued by the title

- Know who I am and enjoyed previous encounters

- Someone you like and trust suggested you read it

- Destiny led you here (you *really* need what the pages promise to deliver)

Or were led here by a blend of some or all of the above.

The second question requires a deeper dig. So, here goes. Who am I?

My name is Michael Hayes Samuelson. I use my middle name because it was my mother's maiden name, and her spirit remains a strong influence on how I live and how I view and interact with the world.

I live in Michigan with my incredible life partner, Hillary, who has encouraged and inspired me for over the forty years of our marriage. We have three children, Brent, Derek, and Logan. They are the fabric of my soul, and I love them dearly. With Hillary, we still talk, share, laugh, cry, get angry, and hug. We are truly present in one another's lives. The three will forever be my friends as well as my children, and the same goes for the grandchildren.

As of this writing, we have the names of four grandchildren: Allegra Jade, Christian Michael, August James, and Jimmie Anne. One of the four precious angels, Jimmie Anne Samuelson, didn't complete the journey into this world. God had other plans. One of her ethereal assignments is to serve as a gentle conscience, an inspiration, and a reflective reminder for all of us to embrace life on this planet and to live a life of integrity. She sits on my shoulder as I write this book. Grandpa Sam gives you an A+, sweet little one.

Why should you value what I have to say?

I'll give you my professional credentials, but they are only part of the reason you might find what I say to be interesting and, hopefully, valuable.

For the past forty-plus years, I have delighted in being a professional health educator. I have a graduate degree in education from the University of Michigan. This is my fourth book focused on living and lifestyle issues. Nationally and internationally I speak extensively on health policy and on the art and science of initiating and sustaining meaningful lifestyle change.

As an academic, I've been a lecturer on men's health at the University of Michigan and an adjunct professor of health management at the University of Rhode Island.

One US President, two US First Ladies, two US Surgeon Generals, noted scientists, media personalities, business leaders, and, most importantly, readers like you say nice things about my work.

Forever dedicated to adventure, I've climbed and trekked to mountain summits in Asia, Africa, Europe, South America, Alaska, and the US lower forty-eight. In addition, I hiked the Galapagos Islands—all after the age of fifty and after being diagnosed with and treated for cancer.

How am I like you?

We are the same, you and me, because, like you, I am and have been

- awed by the beauty of a sunrise
- frightened at the prospect and ongoing responsibilities of parenthood
- blessed with wonderful friends
- confounded by the thinking and actions of foolish people, me included
- moved to tears
- very sick and very well
- lucky at love
- devastated by rejection
- buoyed by happiness
- crushed with disappointment
- delighted by good fortune
- discouraged by missed opportunities

- perplexed by age-old imponderables
- questioned some of God's judgments
- humbled by nature
- both a willing and blinded victim of hubris
- both amused and anxious by my father's reflection
- guilty, passionate, lazy, resourceful, self-absorbed, an introvert, and forever hopeful

Like you, I live, breathe, bleed, and ponder. However, perhaps more than most, I pay close attention, and I take notes.

What do I have to say?

Turn the pages, and you will find out. You can do it page by page or jump around at will, whenever you wish.

What do I want you to do?

Nothing. No action required or requested. My guess, however, is that, like Lao Tzu's empty vessel, you will fill the structure that follows with what's meaningful to you.

> Thirty spokes share the wheel's hub;
> It is the center hole that makes it useful.
>
> Shape clay into a vessel;
> It is the space within that makes it useful.
>
> Cut doors and windows for a room;
> It is the holes which make it useful.
>
> Therefore profit comes from what is there;
> Usefulness from what is not there.
>
> —He who is known as Lao Tzu, sixth century BC

I wrote this book to capture and preserve emotions, observations, and learning gathered on the journey that began with the words, "Michael, you have cancer," a journey that continues today.

This journey shocked and shook me away from a life that could have been one of Thoreau's lives of quiet desperation. I could have gone to my grave with my song still in me. Instead I live a life of texture and color. A life, not marked by survival, but one marked by thrival.

Since 2001, I've given scores of talks around the country about my mountain adventures following diagnosis and treatment. The theme of my talks is life beyond survival. It is about living a life of thrival.

About that word, *thrival*. I thought I made it up, but it seems others had similar epiphanies about surviving beyond survival. There is a usage with this definition in the online *Urban Dictionary*: "adjective for looking beyond your soul into the deepness of society's problems; sacrificing yourself and going beyond one's comfort zone in order to help the people around you." Works for me.

Also, I wrote this book in response to my experience asking my father a series of questions over the past thirty years:

- Dad, what did you think about _____?

- And, Dad, when you were my age _____?

- Well, how about _____?

- And _____?

Unfortunately, they were quiet, one-sided conversations. My dad died thirty-eight years ago. He was just about my age when he died, sixty-seven.

Dad, I wanted to know the answers to these questions:

- I'm thinking about starting my own business. What do you think?

- Another baby on the way. Whoa. What do I do now?

- Any tips for not going crazy being away from home, living out of a suitcase?

- How do I fix this broken windowpane?

- What was my grandfather like? Were you and he close? How about your mom?

- In this picture, who is the funny-looking guy with the handle-bar mustache?

- What was it like to live through the Great Depression?

- Did you know about the concentration camps?

- What did you do in Montana with FDR's Civilian Conservation Corps?

- What went through your head when you were told you had lung cancer?

- How did you get booze during Prohibition?

- Yours was a time of segregation, Jim Crow, and open racism. How did you feel about that?

- What can you tell me about our heritage?

- What was your biggest regret? Your greatest joy? What were your darkest fears?

- Did you believe in God? Why?

- What did you do when you were afraid that you couldn't make the house payment?

- Another baby, two boys and a girl. Wow, you had four kids! How did you do it?

- Dad, if you had a life do-over, what would you do over?

- We think Hillary is starting menopause. Any advice?

- How did you keep it together when my sister, your daughter, died that horrible night in a hotel room in Ann Arbor?

No response.

Hmm? So I told my kids to ask me questions *now*, before, well, you know, before…

Nothing. Not a single question. Then I got to thinking, wait a minute. They don't know what they don't know! These kids are in their thirties. It's not their responsibility to lead with the questions, it is my responsibility to lead with the answers.

I also thought about the next generation, the grandkids. I wanted them to have the resource when they thought to themselves or asked their parents, "What would Grandpa Sam say about _____?"

So this book was born. This is a book of lessons and reflections from my cancer journey wrapped in a memoir of essays and poetry about life, in general.

When I tell audiences, all audiences, not just cancer audiences, about this book project, the enthusiastic response is, I want to read that book! Honestly, I think it is the title, *Beyond Cancer Survival: Living a Life of Thrival,* that appeals to them. After all, who wants to simply survive each day?

INTRODUCTION

What's it all about, Alfie?
Is it just for the moment we live?
What's it all about when you sort it out, Alfie?
Are we meant to take more than we give
Or are we meant to be kind?

—Bert Bacharach

WHEN DIONNE WARWICK SANG THIS SONG IN 1966, I WAS AN anxious and confused recent high school graduate that summer in Ann Arbor, Michigan. And I wasn't alone.

The blush of the sixties was deepening on the face of America. The Civil Rights movement was in full swing. Mao published his *Little Red Book*. Timothy Leary urged us to "turn on, tune in, and drop out." Protest movements were becoming a regular occurrence on US college campuses. Vietnam was heating up, and draft cards and the state of Mississippi were burning.

Also, lost behind the *New York Times* headlines and Uncle Walter Cronkite's lead stories on the CBS News was the ground breaking for twin Manhattan skyscrapers called the World Trade Center. These twin towers symbolized the crest of a Wall Street bull market wave that started in 1949. It was a time of surging passive wealth, spreading economic disparity, and smoldering social unrest.

The songs of the day reflected the mood of the nation. We were all scratching our heads and asking Alfie what it was all about. Buffalo Springfield spoke for a generation when they observed, "There's something happening, what it is ain't exactly clear...nobody's right if everybody's wrong." And Bob Dylan told us "the times they are a changin.'"

One thing was for sure; Dylan was right; the times were, indeed, changing.

I was standing in the doorway, blocking up the hall. Stalled. One semester at Eastern Michigan University made it crystal clear that I didn't have the focus, sense of direction, or discipline needed for college. Not yet. A job in the Detroit auto plants held little appeal. Happiness and success lay somewhere down the road from Ann Arbor and Ypsilanti, Michigan—somewhere over Dorothy's rainbow.

With Dylan's words embedded as both anthem and compass, I set out to discover my passion and purpose. Following a portion of Dr. Leary's advice, I dropped out of school and joined the US Air Force.

The summer of 1967 found me at Myrtle Beach, South Carolina, literally "sitting on the dock of the bay," as Otis Redding sang.

All should be perfect. The waves slosh against the creaky dock. A rainbow slips in behind the morning mist. The Busch beer bought at the Base Exchange is cheap and cold. The girl from North Wilkesboro is innocent, sexy, engaging. Otis sings, "Watching the tide roll away." The sun warms my body, but a quiet ache blurs the rainbow and snuffs the joy out of this and so many other possibility moments. All I hear is Otis, "Wastin' time."

I'm nineteen years old during what would later be called the Summer of Love. Well, I can't seem to focus on love, and, unlike Otis, I'm not "resting my bones." I'm continuing my blind and frenetic scurry down an increasingly cluttered, anxious, and confusing path. Like so many others at nineteen or twenty-nine, thirty-nine or sixty-nine, this sixties stop, along with a series of stutter steps to follow, is more about retreat than quest.

The past and the future merge on that Myrtle Beach day. I don't know what I'm running to, and, other than loneliness, I only have a vague sense of what is chasing me. The one thing I believe for sure is that, like Otis, I'm wasting precious time.

It would be many years before I even sniffed the truth. The truth that real treasures, unlike transient and superficial end points, objects, and the whims of others, are beyond tangible. They are airy. And they are quicksilver. The treasure, this gift, is not a stagnant something waiting for us at the end of the journey. Gifts and opportunity accompany every step—just waiting for discovery. Gifts such as precious time spent sitting in the morning sun watching the ships roll in, the gift of cold beer on a hot summer day, Otis singing my song, the kiss and the warm blush of a beautiful girl on a hot summer day.

Success, like happiness, cannot be pursued; it must ensue, and it only does so as the unintended side effect of one's personal dedication to a cause greater than oneself or as the by-product of one's surrender to a person other than oneself. Happiness must happen, and the same holds for success: you have to let it happen by not caring about it.

—Viktor Frankl

I love these words from Frankl's *Man's Search for Meaning*. It sums up the theme of this book perfectly. Also, in addition to loving Frankl's words, I urge you to remember to protect the joyful memory and innocence of Orson Welles's Rosebud and appreciate the everyday gifts of Thornton Wilder's Grover's Corners. Do not push away gold while reaching for tin. Tend to the soulful needs of the poet while meeting the corporal needs of the pragmatist.

The pragmatist sees the road, the poet sees the journey
One has definition, the other promise without boundaries
The pragmatist avoids the rocks, the poet picks them up
One expects danger, the other hopes for treasure
The pragmatist looks at his watch,
the poet looks at the sun
One marks life by carefully measured ticks,
the other by subtle changes in color

—The Poet and the Pragmatist

Knowledge, passion, purpose, texture, and context yield lasting significance and value. Remember that happiness is a subjective measurement of well-being and that success, as defined by you, ensues from living a socially responsible life accented by personal integrity.

Satisfaction lies in the effort, not in the attainment, full effort is full victory.

—Gandhi

Hey, Dorothy, it's not somewhere *over* the rainbow.
It *is* the rainbow!

39

Reflections from Glaciers, Mountains,
Rain Forests, Boardrooms & Life

THE SCAR

I LOOK IN THE MIRROR AND THERE IT IS. A DIAGONAL LINE, about eight inches, that stretches from my right armpit to my sternum. It's always there. The scar. It's always there.

I remember the date. April 8, 1999, tax time. And that means a last-minute dash to my accountant's office where I am both nervous at the prospect of owing the government more money and anxious to get this annual torture behind me. The office looks the same as it did last year and the year before, and the year before that. The secretary is as friendly as always, and the coffee is as bad as I remember it. As I walk into my accountant's office, I reflect for a moment on how quickly time passes. Wasn't I just here?

Same wrinkled white shirt, same tie askew, same papers piled high on his desk. Yes, it's tax time, all right. Standing up with outstretched hand, Rod smiles his big Irish smile as he greets me. He's the same old Rod, friendly and inviting, but he looks tired. Tired and, well, different.

"How are you?" I ask with more than the usual, everyday courtesy. "Are you okay?"

"Actually," he says, "I just finished my second round of chemo, and I am a bit out of sorts."

A quick tilt of my head tells him that I didn't know about the *what*? Cancer? Yes. He says, reading my face, "I had a modified radical mastectomy in January."

Too much to process. Rod has cancer. And, wait a minute, what did he just say? Modified radical mastectomy? Breast cancer? Rod? A man? Breast cancer? Again, my expression speaks for me as I stare across the desk. He's seen this look before, I can tell.

"Surprised me, too!" he says with a small, thin smile and raised eyebrows.

The tax part of the visit goes quickly as we talk more about *it*. How did you discover *it*? How is the family dealing with *it*? How are you handling *it*? One thing is clear: neither of us thought that *it* could happen to men. After about an hour of this, we stand up, shake hands, I give him a hug and tell him I'll pray for him.

He says thank you and smiles his big Irish smile but, this time, a little less big.

I walk out of Rod's office, down the hall, out the door, down the stairs, out onto the sidewalk, and walk toward my parked car. As I reach for my keys with one hand, I puzzle about how we allow the small things in life to steal our time when time goes by so quickly. With the other hand, I check out my breasts, first the left one then the right one.

Then, I stop dead in my tracks. Behind the right nipple, hard as a rock, about the size of a small pea, I feel something. No pain, but definitely, something.

I smile at the power of suggestion. I mean, what are the odds, right? I just saw my accountant, he shares with me that he has breast cancer, I check myself over and find a lump. Come on, now. What are the odds? What was the likelihood that I, too, had invasive ductal carcinoma? Breast cancer.

In a pathology report issued June 2, 1999, I got my answer: SAMUELSON, MICHAEL, M 51 YRS, DIAGNOSIS: BREAST (RIGHT): INVASIVE DUCTAL CARCINOMA. On June 14, 1999, like my friend and accountant, Rod Byrne, I had a modified radical mastectomy. What are the odds, indeed?

When it comes to breast cancer, men are more likely to die from embarrassment than they are from the disease. In general, men do not like to talk about their health or go to the doctor. Trust me on this one, most men don't like to think about having breasts. Pecs, maybe, but not breasts! So they often ignore the early signs of breast cancer until too late. If my accountant hadn't been comfortable enough to tell me about his cancer, and had I not taken the initiative to seek professional help, it is unlikely this book would exist. Given the fact that I had a Grade 3 tumor (very aggressive growth), the odds are I would have died.

After my surgery, I became certified in technical climbing at the Alaska Guides and Climbing School in Haines. With crampons and ice axe, I trekked across the Davidson Glacier in Alaska with my son Derek. I then trekked to the base camp of Mount Everest in Nepal and the summit of Mount Kala Patar, in 2001. In addition, I reached the summit of Kilimanjaro in 2006 just in time to watch the sunrise over Africa.

In 2011, I headed to South America for a mountain adventure in the Andes of Peru, crossing over the rugged Salcantay Mountain Pass while trekking to Machu Picchu in the land of the ancient Incas. At the time of this writing, I'm sixty-six years old, and I recently returned from a life-changing hiking and photography trip to the Galapagos Islands, 650 miles off the coast of Ecuador.

Why? Well, in part because I moved out of the village of Someday. You know the place, it's where we put off living life because of the *toos*: too old, too poor, too busy, too fat, too tired. Now, as I look in the mirror and see the eight-inch diagonal line that stretches from my right armpit to my sternum, the line that's always there—the scar—I often smile with the realization that the only *too* I know for sure is the fact that life is too short. Life is too short for sleeping, blinking, and nodding my way through the precious moments.

It's time to wake up.

FIRST, YOU MUST DECIDE TO WAKE UP!

Because we are human we do not always do what our mothers taught us to do. We make mistakes. We slip. Sometimes we feel guilty, sad, and remorseful. This is followed by a strong commitment to change—to get back on the right path, to do all those things that Mom, our first-grade teacher, Captain Kangaroo, Bert & Ernie, Grover, Mr. Rogers, and Oprah told us to do.

Unfortunately, just like when on a bike path, once we slip off, we tend to make deeper and deeper grooves in the soft grass and mud. If we stay too long, the grooves just get deeper until we find ourselves in someone else's tracks, someone who slipped off the path long before we came along. Without fast action, we quickly adapt to this new trail. It seems so much easier to just continue along in the mud.

The problem is that we know we are in the mud and that we would be much safer if we could break through the rut and get back on the stable road. However, when we try to leave the sloppy and increasingly dangerous trail, we are intimidated by the bumps as we smack up against the groove's edge. So we settle back into the rut (we'll try again, later). We lack the courage, strength, or will to risk the initial jar, so we stay where we are.

Such is life both on and off a bike path. The difference between life and a bike path is that, on the life path, there are plenty of people willing and anxious to tell you what's good for you, what you need to do to live a healthy, happy, and prosperous life, to get back on the right path. Parents, teachers, priests, rabbis, monks, brahmas, mullahs, your Aunt Betty, Dr. Phil, and the next-door neighbor stand ready to offer (push) advice your way. Mostly, this advice is well intentioned, but it is often general in scope with little or no personal relevance.

The Science of Life and the Art of Living

The science of life is general and objective. Forgoing bad genes and catastrophic events, evidence shows that a life accented by a healthy blend of proper nutrition, physical activity, rest and recovery, intellectual stimulation, emotional support, spiritual engagement, and social interaction tends to be long and relatively free from illness and infirmity. Yes, science can show you how to construct a strong skeleton, but you have to lay down the muscle and tease out the connective tissue that makes your unique system work—for you. You have to provide both context and texture. You are the artist. You are both Pygmalion and ivory.

So, what do you want?

There are countless how-to, self-help books outlining the objective science of life, complete with full-color templates. But only you can explore, discover, design, and nurture the unique, subjective, and deeply personal art of living your life.

The questions are these: What do you want? Where do you want to go? What predictably triggers and sustains those moments when you feel truly happy and satisfied with the life you're living? Is it yoga or deep-breathing exercises? How about the Bible, the Koran, the Torah, or the Four Noble Truths? Is it truly better in the Bahamas? And does it simply take a trip to Jamaica to feel all right? Okay, then, what?

Perhaps, for you, well-being, life satisfaction—happiness, if you will—improves when you read a good book, spend time with your kids, go the movies, buy gifts for your grandchildren, drink a cold beer on a hot summer day, watch television, or work till dawn on a project that comes to life and tickles you each time you give it your undivided attention.

For me, every few years, it's a quiet far-far-away mountaintop, exhausted, sleeping alone in a tent surrounded by strangers who quickly become forever-memory friends. For my wife, it was once the thrill of climbing out of a perfectly good airplane, hanging from the wing strut, letting go, and floating through the sky. Nowadays, for Hillary, it is many activities wrapped in a snuggly warm Nana blanket.

How about you? Of course you want to increase and sustain your life satisfaction, your well-being, but first you must *wake up*! You must become aware and take inventory of what brings meaning to your life, today. You must open all senses and pay attention.

The last section this book will suggest guidelines to help you do just that.

THE GAME OF LIFE

LOOK AT PEOPLE AND, AT ANY GIVEN MOMENT, YOU WILL see faces weighted down by turned pages: *If only I..., I should have..., Why did she...?* Consumed by a funhouse distortion of lost possibilities, they drag forward with wads of nostalgia stuck like bubble gum to their shoes.

To escape the pain, they leap forward to the safe world of Someday. Tomorrow, honest, tomorrow. Well, maybe the next day or, umm, perhaps next week, but soon, I promise. Okay, it probably won't happen next week, but it will, someday...I promise. As the hours pass, they stall between disturbing memories of yesterday and Walter Mitty dreams staged in their personal version of Tomorrowland. As the calendar peels back, they are struck with a nagging sense that something is missing from their lives. That something is called Today, and each day is made up of moments, not years.

In my forty years as an educator and six-point-six decades of living, I have watched, facilitated, and played the game of Yesterday & Tomorrow. I now play the game of Yesterday, *Today* & Tomorrow.

Here's how both games are played:

Yesterday & Tomorrow
(No Children, Please)

First of all, there is an age requirement to play. As small children, we are simply too focused on the moment to be any good at this game of past memories and future possibilities. Childishly (this is a good thing), we go about our days without regard for the past, without pinning our hopes on the future. We believe that our world, as presented, contains all that is necessary to meet our needs and make us happy. We simply use what is close at hand.

When hungry, we put anything we can find into our mouth and spit out what we don't like. When bored, we entertain ourselves with our toes, our voice, crawling bugs, empty boxes, cold oatmeal, the cat's tail, or an imaginary friend. When angry, we throw things and scream until someone pays attention and fixes whatever needs fixing. When tired, we lie down and sleep. And when we gotta go—we go!

Of course, we begin serious training for the game of Yesterday & Tomorrow almost immediately. The immediate world around us directs our decisions: a disapproving look, the warmth and security of a hug, the gritty taste of dirt, a burned finger, the comfort of a smile, the discovery of a sweet tooth, an angry cat with claws. We remember.

Until the age of about three, we use instincts and limited memories to satisfy our quest for happiness. What amuses us? What makes us smile? What causes us pain? How do we get rid of this ache in our tummy? Guilt, regret, and finger wagging *couldas, wouldas,* and *shouldas* do not exist for us. Why? Because, for the most part, these emotions are the products of socialization. They are lessons learned from life's book of expectations and acceptance, the latter being critically important and an integral part of life.

To follow this thought, let's put our child into the world of big people. Quickly, the rules of the game begin to unfold. Crying will work most of the time, but not all the time. We learn that different cries make different things happen. One is good for a hug, another gets our diapers changed; one is good for a game of peek-a-boo, another brings food. If we let out a really loud cry, the big people will do anything we want. A long, whimpering cry gets us our blanket, a stuffed animal, the dancing colors that make music above our crib, and a pacifier, or two, or three. Oh, and if we gurgle a lot and make singsong noises, the big people laugh and seem happy. If we giggle and laugh, they are putty in our hands! We are learning to communicate and manipulate our world.

For the most part, this world is friendly and accommodating (yes, I know that for many children this is not the case, but that discussion is for another time). In this world, there is at least one person who seems to truly care about our needs and gives us a wonderful sense of ourselves; sometimes there are even two or more! We are clearly in control, or at least in high command. We have a fairly small, self-contained, protected world populated by our parent(s), relatives, playmates, and trusted others.

As time goes by (ages three to five), we learn more about how to get attention, how not to get attention, how to make people happy, and how to make people angry. We also learn how to feel bad ("I didn't mean it, Mommy."), sad ("Why did you hit me?"), envious ("I want one, too!"), possessive ("It's my toy!"), guilty ("I'm sorry."), embarrassed, ashamed, and repentant ("It was an accident; I'll be better, honest.").

We are lifted and soothed by memories of fun and play, but we're also beginning to replay the tapes of pain, frustration, fear, and doubt. And we have yet to make it to kindergarten!

The clock moves ahead. We are now in school. Because we were born with this amazing imagination, we sit at our desk, looking out the window, thinking about catching frogs or fighting imaginary dragons or playing with angels in the clouds. The pictures are vivid, the sounds are real, and the feelings are true.

Then, all of a sudden, someone yells our name! It's our teacher and she looks angry (we've learned what this look means). Her forehead is all crinkly, her finger is pointing at us, she's leaning in our direction, and all the kids are looking at us. She's saying something about it not being recess and that we should pay attention. Now she's yelling, clapping her hands, saying that if we can't pay attention, we'll have to change our seat (whatever that means). We're not sure what we did, but it must have something to do with catching frogs, fighting dragons, and playing with angels.

So do we stop using our imagination to create wonderful worlds and limitless possibilities? Not yet. The natural inclination to wonder and dream is still too strong to let go. But to us, newly released into an expanding world, there is clearly something wrong with what we were just doing. This teacher, who is so important in our life, has just yelled at us, and we feel really embarrassed. Well, we will just have to look right at her (that's what it means to pay attention) and, at the same time, catch frogs, fight dragons, and play with angels. She'll never know.

Hey, we just got away with something! Again, the child learns to manipulate her world to, in essence, become (or remain) happy. Clearly, childhood inclinations, desires, and dreams are not always consistent with society's expectations.

As a maturing child and young adult, we have learned that acceptance and gratification require sophisticated communication skills (perhaps manipulation is closer to the mark). Smiles and gurgles won't do the trick anymore. We must anticipate, react, change, adjust, modify, charm, evaluate, compromise, assert, pressure, negotiate, and concede in order to meet our needs.

Okay, fine. If that's what it takes, we can do it!

Certainly, in a very real sense, all of the above are part of a recipe that may bring us a truly happy and fulfilling life. Mixed disproportionately and haphazardly, however, it is more likely to give us a shaky foundation of guilt, anxiety, confusion, projection, paranoia, wishful thinking, regret, and an adult world full of *couldas, wouldas,* and *shouldas.* This being the case, we now have a one-way ticket to the Land of Someday and sterling qualifications to play the game of Yesterday & Tomorrow.

Let the games begin! Now that we have qualified, we can move ahead with the game of Yesterday & Tomorrow.

Actually, the game is quite easy to play. All we have to do is focus on our mistakes while disregarding the nature of being human. At any given moment, should we slip and start to feel good about ourselves, we simply erase that feeling by remembering how inept, undeserving, hopeless, fat, ugly, undisciplined, and stupid we really are. That brings us back to where we belong, and fast. Of course, feeling like a loser can overwhelm even an all-star player, so we fast-forward to the day when we won't be so inept, undeserving, hopeless, fat, ugly, undisciplined, and stupid. Funny, though, the harder we run, the farther away that day seems. But once we do start on the path to change, there comes that moment when we begin to feel good about ourselves, and we all know what that means.

Yesterday, Today & Tomorrow
(Players of All Ages Welcomed and Encouraged to Play!)

Memories of yesterday can be gentle and patient tutors that guide us today, while dreams allow us to set goals and rehearse the success of tomorrow. But these are merely the bookends that outline reality. The living part of life occurs between the two dimensions of past and future. To use an old analogy, they are the grains of sand that pass through the hourglass. Or, more to the point, it is the dash on your tombstone that separates the year you were born from the year that you die.

In order to survive, the developing child needs to adapt, adjust, compromise, negotiate, and learn all the other subtleties of life. However, to *thrive,* she must also hold tightly to her independence, spirit, imagination, zest for living, and respect for life's treasures. When she lets go or has these treasures ripped from her, the bookends gradually collapse until the essence of life, available only in the moment, is squeezed out, leaving the world of *couldas, wouldas, shouldas,* and *somedays.* Gone is the magic of the sunrise; muted are the sounds of laughter; screened are the faces of loved ones. Awe is replaced, at first, by skepticism and finally, if not careful, by cynicism.

Just for fun, let's not disturb the dust of yesterday, and let's put away the crystal ball filled with narcotic dreams of tomorrow. Simply open your eyes and look around. What do you see, feel, hear, and sense in your world? Where do you fit in? Not in the past and not in the future—right now, at this moment. This is where you live. Those other places are merely spun memories and looking-glass dreams.

I encourage you to recapture the wonder of the child who lives in the moment and to run from the analytical adult whose days are filled with doubt and insecurity.

Welcome to my world! Come, let's play.

DEATH IS NOT A CURABLE DISEASE

Swept by the current of the four powerful rivers,
Tied by strong bonds of karma, so hard to undo.
Caught in the iron net of self-grasping,
Completely enveloped by the darkness of ignorance.

—Lama Tsongkhapa

OKAY, SO HERE'S THE DEAL: YOU'RE GOING TO DIE. WE ALL are. Sorry if that comes as a shock and more sorry if you know this but prefer to consider it at a later time.

That notion—that we can deny, ignore, or defer the reality of death—is dangerous, futile, a wasted opportunity, and the height of hubris. And it's just plain stupid. Once conceived, most souls reading these pages will ride the raging rivers of birth, aging, illness, and death. Awareness, acceptance, compassion for our fellow travelers, and the ability to let go of attachments, to let it be, to go with the flow, will determine our level of suffering, our level of well-being.

Here's the really sad part. Many people, when they are healthy and vibrant and not in the throes of advancing hospice care to a loved one, accept the concept of death, a finite existence, only as an intellectual construct. Yes, sure, someday, someday, sure, but not now. Someday.

Here's a fact: Most of us will not die in our sleep after a wonderful fun-filled day of (fill in the blank). For most of us, there will be a period of illness before we die, and, if we are fortunate enough to grow old, there will be the accompanying infirmities that come with time. To quote the Bard from *As You Like It*:

The sixth age shifts into the lean and slipper'd pantaloon, with spectacles on nose and pouch on side; his youthful hose, well sav'd, a world too wide for his shrunk shank; and his big manly voice, turning again toward childish treble, pipes and whistles in his sound. Last scene of all, that ends this strange eventful history, is second childishness and mere oblivion; sans teeth, sans eyes, sans taste, sans everything.

—Jacques (Act II, Scene VII, lines 139–166)

My goal is to shake you out of your slumber so that you can be fully awake before you die. Yes, that's right, most of us are sleeping or shuffling along in that overcrowded village of Someday. Oh, please, you know the place, Someday. The place where, somehow, our once-upon-a-time-soaring-spirits, filled with determination, passion, and world-changing guts, have landed, tail-tucked, and whimpering for fear of…what? Oh, yeah, fear of not meeting someone else's expectations of where we should be or what we should be doing.

Yes, for most of us, Shakespeare's sixth and seventh ages will be a time of physical decline, but it can and *should* also be a time of great joy and satisfaction. This is a time for repose and peaceful reflection on a life well lived. This is the time where Walter Mitty rests not from the angst that comes from a passive life of projection, fantasy, and deferred joy but from the serene fatigue that comes from inhaling a life of active living.

Now that we've got that out of the way, we can focus on the real issue: morbidity. Or perhaps a better way of looking at it, the quality of the dash (-) that separates the date of your birth from the date of your death. The date of your birth is fixed and beyond your control. You are here, so open your eyes to all of it, the good, the bad, and the truly ugly. The other date, your death, is inevitable and is simply a matter for the stonemason.

As they did about so many things, Joseph Campbell and Viktor Frankl spoke eloquently and passionately about the art of living, the dash. When asked about the meaning of life, Campbell would say, "There is no meaning *of* life. We bring the meaning *to* life." He agreed with Frankl's philosophy that sustained well-being (achievement, happiness) ensues from the honorable and enjoyable pursuit of meaningful goals.

Beyond the physical, anxiety in old age often spills from a gunnysack of *wouldas, couldas,* and *shouldas,* a life of regrets. To those who have danced until their feet throb with joy, the quiet of old age is paradise. As Carl Jung once said, "An old man who cannot bear farewell to life appears as feeble and sickly as a young man who is unable to embrace it."

> *Eternity is that dimension of here and now that all thinking in temporal terms cuts off. And if you don't get it here, you won't get it anywhere.*
>
> —Joseph Campbell

PERHAPS YOU ARE MERELY *LOST* IN MIDSENTENCE

I can't explain myself, I'm afraid, Sir, because I'm not myself you see.

—Alice, *Alice in Wonderland*

ALTHOUGH SOME WOULD ARGUE THAT OUR STORY IS already written and that we are simply walking through our predetermined roles, I'm not among them.

That being said, when it comes to the choices we make—how, why, what we decide—I'll concede a portion of the free-will-is-a-myth argument. It's impossible (foolish) to dismiss the impact and minimize the complexity of the genetic, biochemical, social, environmental, and physical determinants that feed the decisions we make. At this very moment, now, this mostly carbon, hydrogen, oxygen, and nitrogen mass of neurons, protons, and electrons called Michael is the sum total of his (its) atomic experience.

Okay, got it. What about the next moment? Is there a point in time where there is an I and I get to call the shots? How about a moment where I get to take the stage for a solo performance while giving a tip of my hat or the back of my hand (depending upon the performance) to my supporting cast of ancestors, butterfly wings, travelers, dopamine surges, and neuroreceptors?

In this cosmic story, am I (Michael) a word, a paragraph, a punctuation mark, an independent or dependent clause? Perhaps I'm merely a work in progress, a partially written sentence created by a multitude of causes put into play before this form of I arrived. That being the case, perhaps I am both an evolving and expanding causation particle in a collective universe as well as a solitary effect innocently stumbling in midsentence—pen in hand, tasked with completing the line—doing the best I can and trying not to get too lost along the journey.

Yes, I am both. I believe in both free will *and* determinism. They are not incompatible. There is no tabula rasa, no virgin canvas or blank piece of paper. I am neither the first nor the sole artist. I do not get to tear off the old sheet and begin fresh. This gift (and, oh yes, it is a gift) came to me filled with scratches, confusing instructions, perplexing designs, horror, and beauty. I also believe that, independent of my conscious wants and desires, this opportunity—to add my mark—is exactly what I asked for and exactly what I need. It is both exhilarating and paralyzing, but it is mine.

If we believe that the absence of optimal well-being and thrival arises from an individual's free-will choices, the actual biological, social, and economic causes will go unexplored and unaddressed. Rather than focus on lack of willpower or individual blame, it's important to figure out how to limit, constrain, and prevent those situational forces that propel us toward harmful choices.

Let me try to simplify this. While you don't have ultimate responsibility (free will), you do have situational or proximate responsibility (accountability).

> But the Hebrew word, the word timshel—'Thou mayest'—that gives a choice. It might be the most important word in the world. That says the way is open. That throws it right back on a man. For if 'Thou mayest'—it is also true that 'Thou mayest not.' Don't you see?
>
> —Lee, John Steinbeck's character in *East of Eden*

I may…and, then again, I may not. It's up to me!

What a wonderfully freeing reality it is to know that, indeed, at the moment of decision, you do have a choice. To deny choice not only condemns you to victimhood, it also negates all of your positive accomplishments and victories—past, present, and future. For, after all, if rain clouds track you down for fierce punishment, how can you possibly control the sun?

It's so easy to deflect accountability for our actions, to cower in the shadow of our own behavior, while we shuffle away murmuring and whimpering, It's not my fault, it's not my fault. If you go through the day blaming Mom or Dad (sister, brother, uncle, aunt, the boss, the boy next door, the Taliban, ISIS, world hunger, Bill O'Reilly, Michael Moore…) for your poor life choices and their consequences, all I can say is get over it!

You can choose to wallow in self-pity, cling to your persecution blanket, and project miserable images of your future, or you can draw lessons from bad experiences and the jerks you've met along the way and move forward. It truly is your choice. Sorry for being so blunt, but I'm growing weak with concern.

Oh, and if you're going for that third hot dog, keep in mind that it's simply because you choose to eat another hot dog. If you prefer, you can blame your dear dead grandmother, who fed you cookies, cakes, homemade jam, donuts, candy, and lots and lots of pasta; nonetheless, you're the one ordering the third hot dog. And if you're an alcoholic and can trace it to the tequila shooters you and your dad used to do when you were fifteen, that's truly tragic. However, you're a big boy now. You're responsible. You're accountable. Push away from the bar.

Need help? Man-up. Seek and ask. There are brothers and sisters standing in the shadows ready and eager to assist.

THE VILLAGE OF SOMEDAY

Don't put off until tomorrow what can easily be put off till the day-after-tomorrow just as well.

—Mark Twain

WHAT IS THIS FEAR THAT PUSHES OUR ONCE CHILDLIKE, playful, carefree glee to the sidelines?

Memories? Early impressions?

Was it Mom's look when you brought home a D in Chemistry? Father Tobin when he caught you sipping sacramental wine? Coach Palmer's frown when you walked-in the winning run? Or maybe it was Gloria Wilson, from history class, who laughed when you asked her if she'd like to go see *My Fair Lady* with you at the Michigan Theater?

Okay, enough about me.

But what causes this transformation from "Let me in, coach!" to "That's all right, I'll just sit over here and watch"? Yes, it's fear of failure, performance anxiety, procrastination, and shyness, but that just gives it a name, it's not an explanation, and it certainly isn't a solution.

Perhaps there is an answer or two found in a story told by violinist Joshua Bell about his experience at the Stulberg International String Competition when he was twelve years old. Much younger than the other competitors, Joshua confesses that he had low expectations for his performance, and, true to his vision, he started out miserably, worse than ever before. Instead of continuing and, in his words, feeling lousy, he stopped, turned to the audience and said, "I'd really like to start over."

Believing that he had already lost the competition, he relaxed, slipped into a zone of confidence and comfort, and played the difficult piece better than ever before. He ended up finishing third in the competition (first the following year), but that was secondary to the lesson he learned about mindset and attitude. Joshua said, "It taught me that when you take your mind off worrying about being perfect all the time, sometimes amazing things can happen. It was a turning point and a lesson I use to this day."

The story—all by itself—is a good one. Quit trying to be perfect, none of us are. However, a closer look at what he is saying shows us something else as well.

The transformation from validating expectations of poor performance to near-perfect playing of the concerto can be found in the two words: *performance* and *play*. We don't tell our children to go outside and perform; we tell them to go and play. In the English lexicon, the opposite of work is play.

When an athletic team wins a major event like the World Series in baseball or the Super Bowl in football, the sheer glee you see in the winners jumping up and down and hugging each other is a demonstration of play, not performance.

Athletes speak of the zone in the same way that Joshua does. Winners focus on feelings of joy that come from within, not outside opinions or expectations—good or bad. I once had a boss who, before I headed out for a major speech or sales presentation, would always tell me to have fun.

All of a sudden, the anxiety would melt, and I would look forward to the event. Have fun! Really? Have fun? Okay, then, I can do that. I can have fun, enjoy myself, and relax. I embraced those expectations without fear of failing to do so.

Perhaps the population of the Village of Someday continues to explode because we view our lives as a performance. A performance under constant scrutiny; critics are standing by, pencil in hand, hoping for a mistake to chronicle. YouTube and all of the social media wait for your viral public and permanent embarrassment.

The next time you feel hesitant about taking a risk while whispering Someday, picture a moment in your life when you leapt into the air with sheer joy. A time when you smiled until your face hurt, giggled uncontrollably, felt deep passionate happiness and contentment. Do that and tell me what word best describes the trigger. Work? Performance? How about play? How about fun?

You can do as the virtuoso performer Joshua Bell almost did—continue on and feel miserable—or you can do as the twelve-year-old boy Joshua Bell did. Stop, turn to anyone who wishes to listen and—beckoning the child inside you—say, I'd really like to start over. And then play. Simply play until your bones shake and your spirit lifts.

Don't perform life. Play and enjoy life, and sometimes—just like Joshua—you'll find that amazing things can happen.

Everything can be taken from a man or a woman but one thing: the last of human freedoms to choose one's attitude in any given set of circumstances.

—Viktor Frankl

RESPECT THE POWER OF SELF-FULFILLING PROPHECY

IN MY YEARS AS A PARENT, TEACHER, COUNSELOR, TRAINER, business leader, cancer patient, world traveler, university professor, and researcher, I've learned that self-fulfilling prophecy is by far the most powerful force in human behavior. If you believe something strongly enough, and if that something is within the realm of possibility, you will do everything possible to make sure it happens. It's that simple, and that powerful.

What occurs is that you begin to see, hear, and feel the predicted outcome—good or bad. You write the script; you rehearse the basic movements; you position the other actors, adjust the lighting, and yell, "Action!"

I have watched brilliant students fail and marginally gifted students rise to the top. I've watched terminal cancer patients live more than fifteen years beyond medical expectations, and I've watched patients with a high probability of long-term survival die shortly after telling me they would.

I've seen physically gifted athletes fail to reach their potential and physically average kids break records. I've listened while individuals accurately predicted doomed marriages, tanked jobs, and lost children. To make matters even worse, the wizards who accurately forecast gloom and doom actually seem to take perverse pride in their ability to predict their failures. Their mantra is, "See, I told you so!"

If you find yourself surrounded by people who use this power in a negative way, I caution you to be careful. They are on a mission, and you may well be part of the script. Instead of following their lead, surround yourself with people who start with positive possibilities, nurture them into probabilities, and then bask in the wonderful realities they create.

Listen to your self-talk and scrutinize the film clippings running through your mind. Are you creating storyboards for a disaster movie or a heroic tale of success and accomplishment?

Reflection 8

PAIN AND SUFFERING: ONE IS A TEACHER AND ONE IS A LEECH

PHYSICAL AND EMOTIONAL PAIN ARE PART OF LIFE AND, unless consciously self-inflicted, beyond our control. Pain is usually temporary; it often serves a diagnostic purpose. A persistent pain in the belly warns of a problem that needs attention. Acknowledging the emotional pain of losing a loved one is part of the healing process.

Having been on the receiving end of both kinds of pain, I know that pain can, at times, be unbearable, requiring medication and lots of support.

Although the words *pain* and *suffering* are often used interchangeably, there is a difference. Pain is a specific emotional or physical reaction to an actual event. I stub my toe, it hurts; her boyfriend leaves her, it hurts; his child is ill, it hurts. And when it comes to emotional pain, flashback moments may pop up years after the actual event. At that moment, the pain is just as real as it was years before.

Suffering, on the other hand, is characterized by its all-consuming presence, tenacity, and debilitating impact ("It's been five years since my boyfriend left me and it still hurts every day.

I'll never find anyone else."). Sometimes the obsessive reaction is based solely on conjecture or fabrication ("If only I hadn't taken this job." "My parents ruined my life." "Nobody will ever understand me." "Things could have been different, if only...").

Pain is involuntary; suffering is by choice. Pain can have value, but, woe-is-me suffering sucks you dry and then moves on to another victim.

Let's take a horrific example: the death of a child. Now, please understand that, as a parent and as a grandparent, I cannot think of anything more painful than this. The sorrow is indescribable; it may go on for months, for years, then return to pierce the heart at intervals throughout the rest of life. However, healthy parents, no matter how intense the pain, eventually move on with their lives, carrying with them both sad and joyful memories. They smile again, they laugh. They're never quite the same; however, they choose not only to survive, but to thrive.

If a grieving parent cannot move past obsessive sorrow, if daily, debilitating pain stretches on for years, they are, at some level, actively contributing to their ongoing heartache. This is not a value judgment; they have every right to do this. However, at this point, either their suffering is by choice, or they have a serious concern that needs professional attention.

Okay, that's the extreme case. But how about you? Are you choosing to carry baggage from years ago? Obsessing over events, conversations, or missed opportunities? If you are, there's no question that you're suffering and that suffering can cause real pain. But please understand that nobody can relieve that suffering, that particular pain, but you. You're choosing to let it drag you down and interfere with your life. This is your right. But is this what you truly want? Does it advance your overall well-being? No judgment, just a question.

Of course, it's not as simple as snapping your fingers and wishing the pain and suffering away. But the first step is to wrestle back control and start thinking differently. Read or reread the section on self-fulfilling prophecy. If you believe strongly enough that change is possible, you will do all that is in your power to make it so. If, on the other hand, you sincerely believe that it is your destiny to suffer—guess what?

NAMASTÉ

WHAT FOLLOWS IS A REFLECTION ON MY TRIP TO NEPAL. THE beacons bear exotic names: Everest, Ama Dablam, Lhotse, and Nuptse. The treasures are new insights into my military service during the Vietnam War, lessons learned from the Sherpas, and my awakening to the mystery of the Divine Thread. This reflection is my attempt to capture moments from an experience that, however elusive, will stay with me forever.

A note about the Vietnam War: As an active member of the armed services from 1968 to 1972, I never set a foot in Vietnam. That said, all of us who wore the uniform were on 24/7 standby. We lived each day to support our brave brothers and sisters stationed in Southeast Asia.

It begins with my flight home, riding in serene comfort 15,000 feet above a rice paddy in Southeast Asia…

My eyes burn. I can hardly swallow. My nose stings. I feel an almost overpowering urge to sob. Not just cry. Really sob.

Why not just let it go? Why not just bawl, weep, bleed—give in and release these jumbled emotions? What is it that fights for control of this fifty-three-year-old man?

As I look down upon the jungle of Vietnam, I wonder: Is this swell of tears summoned by the lingering stench of a war? Or is it merely physical exhaustion from my three-week, 110-mile trek through the mountains of Nepal, a cumulative ascent of over 30,000 feet?

Then again, maybe it's the exhilaration of meeting the remarkable Sherpa culture, followed quickly by the sorrow of having to leave their warm hospitality. Or perhaps it's just a cancer survivor's sense of pure joy and humble gratitude, a heightened awareness and sense of engagement.

The answer, of course, is yes. Yes to all the above, and yes to the many winds and currents of life not yet understood.

The Tokyo-bound Boeing 747 ascends steadily across Vietnam into the clouds over the South China Sea. I rest my head against the window, the slipstream roaring faintly a few inches away; on this side of the clear plastic, a jittering kaleidoscope of emotions wrestles for control of my mind.

I think about aging, the inevitability of change. I think about cultures, how they are neither right nor wrong, just different. I think about the blessings of challenge, the intellectual giddiness and primal fear that come from questioning foundations, values, and social norms.

There is both 'fear and awe in spiritual awakening—in knowing that we are connected, all part of a larger whole: the cursing businessman running to catch a plane at JFK; the first-year teacher struggling to make a difference in a forsaken inner-city school; the battered teenage mother escaping reality through a needle; three young Thai pseudo-Supremes belting out a surreal "Baby Love" in a Bangkok bar; the butcher in Kathmandu proudly hawking hygienic meat; the Vietnam-era veteran in the airliner over the South China Sea.

It begins in the darkness of prehistory and extends into the bright light of the far future. It is the Divine Thread that connects us all.

This spirit of connectedness is acknowledged by millions of citizens of the world—people who, upon meeting, gently bow, form a steeple with their palms pressed together, and offer the greeting, "Namasté." Loosely translated from the Sanskrit, Namasté means, The Divine (or spirit) in me honors and acknowledges the Divine (or spirit) in you. It is pronounced *NAH-ma-stay*.

Namasté doesn't come with a power handshake, superficial hug, or near-miss kiss. It's not "let's do lunch" or "nice car." It's not about social status or material possessions. Namasté is a simple, beautiful recognition of the bonds of life. From Bombay to Boston, children smile at a friendly face. In Cairo or Chicago, a sunset stirs the soul. A hungry child in Kathmandu cries the same as a hungry child in Kalamazoo. Namasté celebrates our common joy and our common pain, the equality and universality of spiritual depth.

In my dawning awareness of the Divine Thread, all the fragments of my life stretch to find their place. How does the spirit of Namasté tie them together? Can this question be answered? Can I live with the answer?

Now I have a choice to make: I can continue to wake up, blinking against the blinding light, or I can close my eyes and drift back into the security of semiconsciousness.

I open my eyes.

Ho Chi Minh. Falling dominoes. Green Berets. Charlie. The draft. Saigon. M-16s. Da Nang. Agent Orange. Public executions. Hanoi. The smell of napalm in the morning. R&R. Buddhist monks on fire. Monkey Mountain. Protesters. Walter Cronkite. Dinner with body bags. "Hell No, We Won't Go." Canada. Burning draft cards. Campus protests. Kent State. Post-traumatic stress syndrome. "Hey, hey, LBJ, how many kids did you kill today?" Police riots in Chicago. The National Guard. Richard Nixon. *The Pentagon Papers.* Paris peace talks. Lyrics: "Four dead in O-HI-O." Peace with honor. Apocalypse now.

I watch the clouds fall away beneath the plane and think of the American kids who never got a chance to grow old, or even grow up. But the clouds make me think of the Vietnamese too—the South Vietnamese and North Vietnamese whose souls were violently separated from their bodies in the same villages where they laughed, made love, comforted their children, retold legends of honored relatives, prayed to their gods, and dreamed of a better tomorrow.

Like most other Baby Boomers, I had been in the habit of intellectually disassociating myself from our generation's war and the wrongheaded decisions of five presidents that had landed us in the quagmire of Southeast Asia. We would shake our heads and sigh: Stupid, senseless, horrific. Immoral. We had become enlightened. We had absolved ourselves, and now we felt cleansed and righteous—that is, until a gnawing sense of the unresolved brought us back into the same discussion, the same pronouncements of moral superiority, the same search for absolution.

When I was a kid growing up in Jamestown, New York, in the fifties and early sixties, the triumph and glory of World War II was still fresh. General Eisenhower became President Eisenhower (I Like Ike!). The Jerusalem trial of Nazi war criminal Adolph Eichmann, the architect of the Holocaust, was broadcast into our living rooms. Theaters still ran war-era cartoons portraying Japanese and German soldiers as buffoons, devils, or both. Clearly the enemy, the ones we had defeated, was not like us. And Joseph McCarthy held Senate hearings trying to ferret out the "communists" among us.

War was fun, exciting, heroic. My buddies and I spent our grade-school afternoons and Saturdays playing war games over on Army Hill just above the Third Street Bridge. We all wanted to be the good guys—the American GIs—but sometimes we had to be the Japs or the Krauts. We fought World War II again and again, and the Americans won it every time.

Oh, there had been another war, in a place called Korea. It was between the Americans and the North Koreans and Chinese. But we kids never fought that one. None of us wanted to play a Commie, and there was some feeling, not spoken aloud, that our GIs were soft and weak and had not distinguished themselves against this suicidal fanatic Yellow Horde.

As young men in high school, we became aware of another race of Commie gooks that needed to be shown how real American soldiers took care of business. My buddies and I would meet the challenge. Unsure about college, feeling invincible and playing movies of John Wayne and Gary Cooper and Humphrey Bogart in our minds, simultaneously exhilarated and frightened, disdainful of the cowardly protesters showing up on campuses nationwide, many of us joined up in hopes of being sent where the action was. Though I wasn't especially eager to go where bullets were flying, I fell into step and marched into the service with my friends. The date was February 1967—just before the war in Vietnam broke wide open.

As President Johnson sent more and more young men into the grinder, both pro- and antiwar propaganda machines went into high gear. I was now a member of the United States Air Force, defender of freedom, protector of the oppressed. Our enemy was the Vietcong—according to our superior officers, Godless gooks who were not like us, who had to be stopped before they spread communism throughout the world.

There were protesters, of course—draft dodgers and hippies and communist sympathizers who insisted I was a tool of an evil military-industrial complex, But I didn't feel that way. I was an airman in the greatest military force in the world. But as the war got bigger, the protests grew louder—and the counterarguments became clearer. Even the popular press began to oppose the war. On February 27, 1968, everybody's favorite uncle, newsman Walter Cronkite, said on the air that the war was mired in stalemate and the only rational way out…would be to negotiate, not as victors, but as honorable people.

More important, my friends were dying or coming back confused and shaken, numbed by the horror and futility of what they had seen. Some who had self-medicated to survive their jungle nightmares came back with drug habits. Many joined the antiwar protests.

By the end of my four years in the military, I was attending antiwar protest rallies at the University of Texas and displaying a peace symbol in the back window of my orange VW Karmann Ghia. I had had enough. And I was not alone; the political tide was shifting. Mainstream America was turning against the war that had taken so many of their fathers, brothers, husbands, and sons for no apparent good.

On January 23, 1973, two years after my honorable discharge, President Nixon announced the agreement to end the war and bring peace with honor in Vietnam. Lyndon Johnson, who had sent nearly 500,000 men and women to Vietnam, died one day before the announcement. On March 29, 1973, the last US ground troops left Vietnam. On April 30, 1975, South Vietnam surrendered to the Vietcong and the army of North Vietnam.

The dead included more than 58,000 Americans, 2.5 million North and South Vietnamese, and 1 million Laotians and Cambodians. Was this enough to make me weep?

Now, as I soar high above the scene of this morally tainted conflict, free of the old fears but still held by the gravity of past horrors, the philosophy of Namasté helps me put it in perspective. Vietnam is as much metaphor as history. When we seek to forgive ourselves this terrible national mistake, we are merely seeking absolution for the crime of being human. Along with beauty, honor, dignity, and compassion, we humans have a great capacity for performing acts that are stupid, senseless, horrific, and immoral. To deny this is to invite it to happen again.

Why did it take me this long to begin to understand the force of Vietnam in my life as an American and a human being? Because when I came to Nepal, I found something I didn't know I was searching for—the Divine Thread. Submerging myself for three weeks in an Asian culture that is both ancient and developing made it easier for me to put my Western arrogance on the shelf and open my heart and mind to another way of life.

I entered the scattered villages of the Khumbu Solo region of Nepal. Not much talk of CNN, MTV, or the NFL; no rosary beads; no landscaped six-lane superhighways with McDonald's at the exits. I found myself in a world of Hindus and Buddhists and prayer wheels, of yak trains on swaying wood-and-rope suspension bridges over rocky river gorges, of rough, grueling mountain paths where, on a good day's trek, you may pass two or three teahouses that will sell you a candy bar and a bottle of water. And yet the citizens of this world, the Sherpas, seem quite content.

As I traveled the narrow mountain pathways, I met porters lugging seventy-pound baskets of wares, balanced by head straps, like generations of traders before them. Passing through villages like Namche, Pheriche, and Lukla, I stopped to bow to villagers and to greet friendly, curious children; to admire the work of stone cutters; to watch priests perform ancient rituals to persuade the gods to bless the crops. Everywhere I went, I met smiles.

Sherpa means Easterner. Over the past five-hundred years, the Sherpas have migrated to Nepal's mountain valleys from Kham, in eastern Tibet. Lamas, with their families and followers, settled in northern Nepal in places with names like Yolmo, Langtang, and Khumbu. Later generations spread south to Sankuwasawa, Ilam, and Charicot, and even as far as Sikkim, Assam, and Darjeeling, in India. Sherpa language, literature, history, philosophy, and religion come from Tibet and Buddhism.

We became acquainted with this fascinating culture in the person of Ang Nima Sherpa, the leader of a spirited and gracious crew from Eastern Nepal. With laughter, song, and compassion, they led us cheerfully and safely through their land.

Like a lost tribe spared the corrosive effects of modern civilization, the Sherpas seem to embody the values and principles suggested in their greeting, Namasté. Their compassion, simplicity, and spirituality are not Hallmark superficial, but innate and instinctive. They seem devoid of ego and pretension.

Perhaps my view of the Sherpas is too idealistic, colored by a traveler's fascination with exotic cultures; but, on reflection, I don't think so. There is something different about the Sherpas, something both real and indescribable. You've seen people work, but when you see the dignity with which Sherpas perform a task, you sense something unique about the way they respect and value work. Although they want and need to be compensated like anyone else, they devote the same attention to all work, paid or unpaid.

You see their unfailing good cheer as they face daily hardships. But what's difficult to measure or describe is the inner peace you sense in their feeling community, their unconcern with the trappings of status.

However cultures may differ, people's basic needs and desires are the same. Courtesy and respect are appreciated; children understand kindness; the soul expresses itself in art; we feel reverence in a spiritual dimension that is undetectable to our basic five senses. This is as true for the inhabitants of Dingboche, Khumbu, and Kathmandu as for those in Hanoi, Da Nang, and Ho Chi Minh City or for the people of Paris, Havana, or Peoria. The Divine Thread links us all.

Is it the joy of the Divine Thread that makes me want to weep?

I experienced ten-hour treks in rough terrain. Thin mountain air. Oxygen starvation.

Headaches. Sleep apnea. Wind. Rain. Sleet. Snow. Sunburn. Sherpa stew, yak momo, and Spam. The Khumbu Krud, a Himalayan biological outrage brought on by high altitude, unfamiliar food, and questionable water. Intestinal parasites, and an utterly alien ecosystem. I was indeed a stranger in a strange land.

Why do we sometimes go out of our way to be uncomfortable? Why do we take on physical challenges that we know will bring pain, make us sick, even threaten our survival? What role do mind and spirit play in physical desire and accomplishment? Does my growing awareness of the Divine Thread that connects me with the Sherpas make me want to share their stoic endurance of hardship? Is my trek across the spine of the Himalayas my homage to the Sherpas' long march from eastern Tibet? Perhaps this is, after all, the path to enlightenment, to recognition of a realm beyond temporal existence. Perhaps this is the price.

Shivering in my sleeping bag, high above a quiet village south of Everest, I ponder these great questions. I crawl out of my tent. I look down at the pinpoints of light that mark homes and villages far below. I look up at the brilliance of the stars above. I begin to understand.

I believe that the answer is indeed our collective search for the Divine Thread. It is the missing element in most of our lives, the lack of which keeps us from feeling part of something greater than ourselves, greater even than the sum of all people. We don't find it in our secure, predictable daily lives, so we push beyond the comfort zone and stumble blindly into uncertainty. Some accumulate wealth and material treasures and find only more emptiness; others seek nirvana through drugs and alcohol and reach a bitter dead end. Most, however, give up the search early and retreat into what Thoreau described as a life of quiet desperation.

But it was this search that led me to the streets of Kathmandu and the mountains of Nepal, and that pulls me even now in other directions beyond guaranteed comfort and security. In the coming months and years, I will again experience physical challenges that will make me sick, bring pain, and perhaps threaten my life. But these same challenges will make me well, give me great joy, and enrich my everyday existence. They will, as well, strengthen the Divine Thread that connects my mind, body, and spirit with all mankind.

For our high-visibility heroes, it is without question the Divine Thread that lets them reach such heights. Yes, they have developed natural physical gifts and talents, but it is their spirit, their positive approach to life, that distinguishes them from Thoreau's desperate masses.

But it's not just the famous who surpass. Ordinary people take on extraordinary challenges outside the comfort zone, enriching their lives and bringing new inspiration to those around them. On the road to Everest, I was lucky enough to meet several such everyday heroes.

One was Ann, a forty-seven-year-old woman from Wisconsin. Ann has asthma. Now, keep in mind that as you ascend through 17,000 feet in the Khumbu region, each breath brings you only half the oxygen you get at sea level. Okay, now think of trekking up to ten hours a day over miles of jagged rocks at grades reaching 12 percent—with asthma! Oh, and another thing about Ann: the year before, she was diagnosed with multiple sclerosis.

Most MS patients experience muscle weakness in their extremities and difficulty with coordination and balance. Most people with MS also exhibit paresthesia, transitory abnormal sensory feelings such as numbness or pins and needles. Some may experience pain or loss of feeling. About half experience difficulties with concentration, attention, memory, and judgment.

So I asked: "Ann, what are you doing walking rocky paths rarely wider than a Wisconsin sidewalk overlooking vertical drops into nothingness?" She straightened, tilted her head up ever so slightly, looked me in the eye, and said, "Michael, I don't want to miss a single dance."

Adventurous does not mean foolhardy, of course. Ann was well prepared for the journey, and she was accompanied by her attentive and caring husband, Michael; her seventy-two-year-old father, Fritz; and her brother, Paul. Fritz and Paul are experienced mountaineers, familiar with such peaks as Rainier and Kilimanjaro. Fritz, who lives near Ann and Michael, had trained her rigorously for months, to good effect; there were days when I couldn't keep up. And she knew her limitations. On two occasions—climbing to the summit of Kala Patar and trekking to Everest base camp—Ann opted out. Her husband stayed with her. Both understand that fulfillment comes when we attach ourselves to activities, not outcomes.

Our expedition was divided into two groups, the Rabbits (fast) and the Grandpas (slow). While I protected the Grandpas' flank, Fritz set the pace and tone with the Rabbits. Ann's father had a stride that said get the hell out of my way! But a temperament as gentle as a late-afternoon Khumbu mist. He was experienced, knowledgeable, dignified, and always ready to help others. I now have a new model for aging.

I will also remember Steve's smile. A young diabetic from Alberta, Steve is a positive young man of twenty-four who trekked to base camp as part of an awareness campaign for the Canadian Diabetes Society. Not much is known about the effects of altitude on diabetes, so Steve took to the hills, injecting his insulin, checking his blood sugar, and recording it all in his journal.

Steve was a pleasant and uncomplaining travel companion. At Everest base camp, he and his twin sister, Shanna, introduced me to three other Canadians, also involved in the diabetes awareness effort, who would attempt to climb Everest: their father, Leo; their brother, Daryl; and Dave, a close family friend. On Thursday, May 24, 2001, Daryl, twenty-eight, became the youngest Canadian to summit, and Dave became the only Canadian to reach the top twice.

In a matter of days, we who started as a loose band of nodding strangers became a family. Steve, Fritz, Ann, Michael, Paul, Shanna, and me, along with Sherri and Gary, sharing more of our lives than we would have ever expected. We made hundred rupee bets on dessert (fruit cocktail vs. pears), compared oxygen saturation readings, and shared breathtakingly intimate details of our gastrointestinal adventures as though we were lifelong friends.

Our Sherpa brothers, Ang Nima and his staff, showed compassion and caring beyond anything I've ever experienced: the loving way they helped Ann over high rocks, their looks of concern when Gary needed extra support, the time Ang Nima reached to carry my backpack before I even realized I needed help. Their unspoken message, always: We are one and the same. It doesn't surprise me that the only time I shed tears on my Himalayan trek was the evening I said farewell to Ang Nima Sherpa and his crew.

I felt I was saying goodbye to both innocents and innocence. I prayed that they would not go the way of so many other cultures and lose their souls to the siren call of satellite phones and cyberspace.

We created many memories in the mountains, many of which bring to mind imaginary book titles—*Small Children with Folded Hands; Washing Water; Prayer Flags, Stupas, and Monasteries, Psycho Porter; A Cup of Chang.* We shared hardships (which were, of course, nothing compared with those of the climbers we met in base camp who were bound for the top of the world), and we shared joys and triumphs that were top of the world on our own scales. Most of all, we bonded in the spirit of Namasté.

In twenty-three days I traveled 21,000 miles through the air; walked 110 miles through wind, rain, sleet, and snow; climbed more than 30,000 vertical feet; suffered oxygen deprivation, sunburn, and the Khumbu Krud. I brought back the physical aftereffects, but more: the many faces of Ama Dablam, perhaps the most beautiful mountain in all the world; the view from Kala Patar; cloud formations beyond the most extravagant imagining; the rhododendron forest, runaway yaks, singing porters; spooky stories of the Yeti; and the smiles of Sherpa children.

What was it that made me want to cry as I flew heavenward toward home? Was it the wonder of it all? Or was it simple exhaustion?

Before I was diagnosed with cancer in 1999, I rarely crossed the boundary between comfort and discovery; now I race to keep up with my expanding awareness. Before my surgery, I viewed life's impermanence as unsettling and abstract; now I smile at the whimsical changeability of life and I honor the moment. Before treatment, I was blissfully unaware of my body's vulnerability; now I cherish the fragile gift of being a human. Before I became a survivor, I undervalued the spirit; now I depend on it to show the power of the possible.

When I thought of them at all, I once saw my mind, body, and spirit as distinct, independent entities. Now I am beginning to see that they are one and the same, one of the millions of fine strands that make up the Divine Thread, and that this thread touches everything and is without beginning and without end.

Cancer is as much a part of Namasté as a Sherpa's calm smile, or the taste of Mackinac Island fudge, or kids with puppies, or the weddings and funerals of lifelong friends. All these things are spiritual nudges that whisper to us: Moments…not years.

Cancer does, of course, mean physical pain and mental anguish, not only for the patient but also for caregivers, friends, and family. Cancer is not easily accepted as a gift, but people are often better for the experience, even those who must bury the bodies and console the loved ones.

The tears finally came, one week after my 747 flew over Vietnam. They caught up with me in Michigan, the day my daughter, Logan, now thirty-two, graduated from Saline High School, the last of our three children to close that particular life chapter. Brent was first, in 1994, and Derek in 1999.

Watching her receive her diploma with an expression that said, "Bring it on, world!" filled me with thoughts of a precious little girl, hope for the future, and prayers of thanks for being there to see it.

Even as I lived in that moment, my mind also drifted back across the Pacific to rice paddies, monsoon rains striking high-mountain trails, porters carrying heavy loads to distant markets, Sherpas reunited with their families. Namasté, I thought: the strong and everlasting, yet precious and fragile, Divine Thread of life.

Let it be said that when given the choice to dance or sit it out, I am like my friend Ann: I don't want to miss a single dance. And I encourage, I implore, I beg you, don't miss a dance. Let the full spectrum of life wash over and through you.

Namasté.

IN THE PROCESS OF BECOMING, DON'T FORGET TO SIMPLY BE

IN *THE WIZARD OF OZ*, IT TAKES A STORM AND A GOOD KNOCK on the head to make Dorothy realize that life's real treasures are not found at the end of a yellow brick road. In fact, as Dorothy discovers, you never even have to leave home. No need for long journeys, strange companions, favors from Munchkins, fights with flying monkeys, witches of any kind, great sacrifices, and all-knowing wizards. All you have to do is open your eyes and look around.

Here's a nice irony, our favorite part of the movie is really Dorothy's big mistake. How she longs to travel over the rainbow. Hey, folks, put away the hankies. Remember the guy behind the curtain? The treasure is the rainbow! And the answers lie in the journey, not at the end of the yellow brick road. For those who pay attention, the answers are on the road and in the scenery alongside the road. Open your eyes, enjoy it, and quit spending your time running from the witch's cackle while chasing imaginary pots of gold. Life is in front of you—today, this moment (and that includes your little dog too).

Many people spend so much time seeking the great and powerful Oz that they miss the wonders and magic of life's journey. When they eventually discover that it's only the charlatan, Professor Marvel, behind the curtain, it's often too late. Their health is ruined, they're sleeping with strangers, and their children have grown up and moved away—emotionally as well as physically. In their quest to become, they forgot to be.

There is a distinct difference between those who mark time in years and those who mark time in moments. Those who check off years miss the journey. Freeze-frame moments have independent value. They are complete in and of themselves, requiring little more than our presence and focus.

Look at your little girl's smile and then name your selling price. What would tempt you to trade away even one hug from a grandchild? Is there a stock with market value equal to a photo album filled with family memories?

In contrast, a life of constant guilt, blame, and pursuit consumes enormous amounts of physical resources and emotional energy. The reward? The rewards are bitterness and perishable hard goods. And this life of years has a perpetually moving end point. Eventually it does end—at its own pleasure, not yours.

Here are a few questions to ponder: Are you running down some path so fast that you've forgotten why you're running? Do you push aside gold as you reach for tin? Do you realize you have a choice? Oh yes, you do have a choice. Some of you are just too busy blaming others, chasing pots of gold, or trying to figure out how to get over the next rainbow to notice. As Dorothy once asked the Scarecrow, "What would you do with a brain, if you had one?"

Sorry for that last snide question. It's just that I've seen too many nice Scarecrows get torched.

CHOOSE WISELY WHEN IT COMES TO HAPPINESS AND PLEASURE

When I was a kid going to Catholic school in the 1950s, there was a high premium placed on suffering. The more you suffered, the faster you washed away your sins. If your account was in good shape, you could shift the surplus value of your suffering over to some poor soul in Purgatory who would then get some time knocked off his or her sentence. You were reinforced for choosing to suffer.

If you went around too long with a smile on your face, the nuns suspected the worst.

"What have you been up to, Michael?" asks Sister Mary Louise.

"Nothing, Sister," I reply.

"Well, then," says the good Sister, "wipe that smile off your face."

"Yes, Sister. Sorry, Sister."

If signs of happiness brought scrutiny, outright displays of pleasure put you directly on a paved road to hell. Or, at a minimum, guaranteed you an extended stay in Purgatory. Then it would be your turn to depend on some nice kid offering up some really good suffering to reduce your sentence.

In spite of a series of Sister Marys, I grew up pretty happy, and I'm still happy. I probably have more than my fair share of pleasure as well. The important thing is to know the difference between happiness—well-being—and pleasure, and when to choose one over the other.

Happiness is strictly a state of mind. It is subjective. What makes me happy may or may not make you happy. However, as long as the source of my happiness is not harmful to others or myself, it is a desirable state and, for the most part, benefits everyone around me. When I'm happy I have more energy, I'm fun to be around, and I tend to be more generous than when I'm not happy. My being happy is a good thing.

In the moment, pleasure is also good. However, it may or may not contribute to my overall happiness or well-being. It's important to think about this before submitting to temptation.

Here's a simple example: Is eating a piece of chocolate cake pleasurable? Yes, certainly. Will it bring me happiness? Yes, I think so. Can't hurt. Well then, how about a whole cake? Will eating a whole cake be pleasurable? Probably, until I'm stuffed. But will it bring me happiness? Nope. The feeling of pleasure will quickly wear off and I'll be left with regret, awakened fat cells, and a nasty sugar crash.

Here's another: Will paying my taxes bring me pleasure? Not a chance. Will it contribute to my overall happiness, my overall well-being? Yes, I can stop worrying about it and keep the IRS off my back for another year.

Simple examples, but you get my point. When next facing a choice with serious consequences, ask yourself: Will this choice make me happy, advance my well-being? Yes? Good! If it also brings you pleasure, that's a bonus. If it brings pleasure but is a threat to your overall well-being, proceed with great caution.

Better yet, sit down, have a piece of chocolate cake, preferably a small piece, and think long and hard before you proceed. If you don't think in terms of short- and long-term consequences, you may need a whole bunch of nice kids with clean slates willing to suffer on your behalf.

VICTIM OR MASTER— YOUR CHOICE

IT'S NOT MY FAULT. HE DID IT. NOBODY TELLS ME ANYTHING. *Why me? I can't help it. If you had to work with my boss… If you had to live with… You don't know my mother.* And on and on and on.

This kind of talk and attitude leads to the most destructive form of self-fulfilling prophecy: Personal pity scripts painted with a broad brush of failure.

It's the song of the classic whiner, the one who seeks out pathos and proudly wears his victim badge. As long as he can find someone to blame, he can live in the past and never take responsibility for his actions. You know him, we all do.

Once you become a whiner, you'll find it hard to break away from victim mentality. You've got lots of companionship because it's such a large club. You never have to look far to find other whiners. Water coolers, talk shows, cable news, airplanes, bars, bowling alleys—everywhere you turn, you'll find someone ready to complain about how life just ain't fair. It's the new national pastime.

Yes, there are injustices, inequities, repression, and suppression. If this is your history, I am truly sorry that you have experienced trauma and pain. You have a right to express your anger, frustration, and hurt. I also recognize your need to curl up in a dark corner now and then and lick your wounds. Licking wounds is healthy and natural—but don't take off all the skin and leave open sores. And don't make it a lifestyle, you'll be miserable and so will everyone around you.

Recognize your role in creating potentially distressful situations. Constantly blaming others, including the universe, will eventually alienate you from your friends, family, and coworkers. You have plenty of control over how you react to challenges. Refusing to accept accountability, or to accept reality—independent of personal accountability—suggests that you don't have control over your life. This makes you vulnerable to distress.

In researching and writing the book *Voices from the Edge*, I had the privilege and honor of meeting and becoming friends with a lot of folks in the cancer community. Many of them were patients experiencing horrific pain, living with the knowledge that today's sunset might be their last.

None, however, considered themselves victims. They were survivors who became thrivers, committed to squeezing out every sweet drop of life that they can. One, Tim Harbour, was told, many years before he died, that he had eighteen months to live. Tim had other plans. Was he in pain? Oh yes. He was disabled from multiple surgeries. Was Tim depressed and frustrated? Sometimes. Looking for sympathy? Don't you dare!

You see, every day that he lived Tim chose to be the master, not the victim. And, while his body was losing the physical battle, his spirit, his soul, remained in control until his last dying breath. This is freedom.

Watch one of several reality shows, then switch off the tube and think about real life. Think about Tim, or someone like Tim. Now decide: In whose neighborhood do you wish to live: *The Real Housewives of New Jersey* or Tim's?

LISTEN TO THE WISDOM OF OTHERS

ONE OF THE KEYS TO SUCCESS IN MOUNTAINEERING and trekking is listening carefully to the lessons learned from others. When experienced mountaineers tell you the type of gear you will need above 17,000 feet, you listen and heed their advice. When they tell you the importance of using a rest step every inch of the last mile to the summit, you listen and heed their advice. When they urge you to drink that fifth liter of water even when you don't think you can take another swallow, you listen and heed their advice.

Keep in mind the fact that great leaders, in all walks of life, quickly learn that they do not have all the answers. More than accept, they embrace the reality that they do not know what they do not know. Before they assume a leadership role, they surround themselves with experienced people and let them talk while paying close attention. They are students. Intellectual curiosity drives and guides them. They put aside ego, eliminate hubris, and replace both with perpetual beginner's mind.

If you are a leader, you've risen to this position not because you are the happening—you got here because you make things happen. Continue to read, ask questions, seek out predecessors' perspectives, and value collective judgments. Final decisions may rest with you, but don't make them in a vacuum. Beyond survival, team thrival demands that you seek knowledge and that you are approachable and open to input. Also, wisdom does not necessarily correlate with age and life station. Fight arrogance and hubris!

Listen to the words of the sixth-century BC Chinese philosopher Lao Tzu: "The wicked leader is he who the people despise. The good leader is he who the people revere. The great leader is he who the people say, 'We did it ourselves.'" Pay attention!

A perfect example of this comes from my Khumbu experience in Nepal with Ang Nima Sherpa. After several days of trekking at high altitude, it became increasingly clear to Ang Nima that I was starting to fade, and quickly. In his gentle, calm, but clearly in-control manner, he approached me, bowed slightly, and asked me to give him my backpack. I smiled, bowed back, and said, "Oh, no thank you, Ang Nima, I'm fine."

Without a smile but still very gentle and in control, he responded, "Michael, give me your pack."

Again, I smiled my strong Western-world smile of denial and said, one more time, "No, really, I'm fine."

And, once again, Ang Nima simply said, "Michael, give me your pack."

Thank God he asked (gently demanded) a third time that I give him my pack. I was exhausted but refused to give in. He knew all the signs, and his steely, quiet determination that I drop the pack was a product of many times up and down the path from Lukla, Nepal, to the Mount Everest base camp. For three days, Ang Nima carried his and my pack up the ragged and exhausting trail with its increasingly thin air. On the fourth day, without announcement, he leaned my backpack outside my tent. I was stronger, ready to carry my own load, and he knew it.

I was so impressed and pleased by what Ang Nima had done. I asked our US guide, Jeff, what would be an appropriate gesture—an additional $100? $500? My Western thinking was that he deserved a huge tip for what he had done. Jeff quickly responded that Ang Nima would be confused by the gesture.

"He didn't help you, Michael, for $100 or for $500. He helped you because in his world you and he are the same person. He carried your backpack because he had the strength and energy and you didn't," Jeff told me.

"You mean," I only half-jokingly replied, "he wasn't showing compassion just for money, that he wasn't holding back his best every day just so that he could provide additional service when he believed there would be extra rupees coming his way?"

Jeff only smiled. "Michael, Ang Nima wouldn't even understand the questions."

Of course my mom taught me all this stuff when I was a kid. How we are all one and the same, part of a collective energy that rises and falls according to each and every person's contribution to our common concerns and shared well-being. I didn't have to go to Nepal to learn that. Perhaps, however, I needed to go to Nepal for the reminder.

By the way, what was the most important thing that Ang Nima did? He gave me back my pack.

Did I reach the Mount Everest base camp, the Khumbu ice falls, and the summit of Mount Kala Patar? Yes. And I did it myself!

Thanks, Ang Nima.

Sherpa: A member of a traditionally Buddhist people of Tibetan descent living on the southern side of the Himalaya Mountains in Nepal and Sikkim. In modern times Sherpas have achieved world renown as expert guides on Himalayan mountaineering expeditions.

—Merriam-Webster

Wellness Sherpa: A health and lifestyle guide who helps you navigate life's metaphoric falling ice, Yetis, crevasses, creaky walking bridges, charging yaks and the Khumbu Krud. Equally important, the wellness Sherpa reminds you to check out life's sundogs, rhododendron forests, crystal-clear night skies, and the power of the possible.

—Michael H. Samuelson

Speaking from my personal experience trekking to the Mount Everest base camp and inching my way breathlessly to the summit of Mount Kala Patar in the Khumbu region of Nepal, I can tell you that the Sherpa people are kind, helpful, intelligent, good-natured, resourceful, compassionate, patient, and tenacious. This view is shared by virtually everyone who has spent time with these high-mountain guides.

The Sherpa reputation for heartiness, experience, and expertise is such that the word *Sherpa* has evolved well beyond the Tibetan definition of Eastern people. Today, the word is used to describe exemplary service and personal attention. There are guides and then there are Sherpa guides—the very best. In life, all sectors, I urge you to adopt the spirit of the Sherpa.

TURN ON YOUR RADAR AND KEEP IT TURNED ON

Knowledge is the true organ of sight, not the eyes.

—Panchatantra

RARELY ARE WE OBLIVIOUS TO THE ROCKS ALONG OUR LIFE path. We are, however, reluctant to lift them to see what lives beneath—even when we sense creepy, crawly, slimy dangers that may attach, follow, and cause us harm. Instead of lifting the rocks to determine risk (or reward), we whistle in the dark and pretend they don't exist.

Lift up the rocks. If there are creepy, crawly, slimy dangers, you have two options: You can always carefully put the stones back in place and pretend you never saw anything, or you can do something about it. It's up to you. Oh, and one more thing, once you pick up the rocks, you can never again be a victim. Welcome to the world of informed responsibility.

As a writer, I find metaphor and simile to be highly efficient ways to advance a story line or drive home critical themes. Radar is an excellent example. In 1969, when war was raging in Vietnam, I was a young airman stationed at the top of Indian Mountain, an extinct volcano in the middle of Alaska. The purpose of radar is to allow you to detect and track incoming objects as early as you possibly can. Radar enables you to determine the degree of threat and, if needed, to take appropriate action.

Every Tuesday morning around 2:00 a.m., a Russian bomber or two would enter our airspace, and the klaxon screamed. Somebody would shout, "The Russians are coming, the Russians are coming!"

Russian bombers crossed into Alaskan air space. We would then notify the Alaskan Air Command in Anchorage, and they would scramble fighter jets to chase the Russians back home. The next night, some young kid who looked like me but spoke Russian would yell, "The Yanks are coming, the Yanks are coming!"

We would then send B-52s into their air space. In response, Russian MiG fighter jets would intercept and escort them back to Alaska.

This game seemed pretty silly until you realized that people in Seattle did not know what was happening. Nor did people in Chicago, Detroit, or Boston. They did not need to know. Somebody was paying attention; somebody was on guard so that others could rest and safely go about their business.

Can you imagine if instead of watching for incoming blips and proactively responding to the possible threat, we decided that we were too busy? Or that we decided that Yukon, Anchorage, or

Seattle would eventually pick up any real threats? How about if we concluded that it was probably just another false alarm? Of course, that would have been crazy, irresponsible, and disastrous thinking. However, we constantly do this in our personal and professional lives.

Apply radar to your life. If you are like most people, you often sense threat but delay taking action because

- You tell yourself that you are too busy.

- You hope that somebody else will deal with the problem.

- You convince yourself that the problem doesn't exist.

Then, as the blips of life get closer and new ones appear on the horizon, your anxiety increases as you continue to convince yourself that you are too busy. You maintain the delusion that someone else will take care of the mounting issues. And you hold on to the notion that the concerns aren't that bad or that they don't exist, at all.

Then the day comes when you look up at the sky and find that the sun is entirely obliterated by threatening blips. Work, health, family concerns, relationships, money problems—they all block the sun. Then what do you say? Well, all too often we express surprise and shock as we tell everyone and ourselves, I didn't see that coming!

Of course, you did. You saw it way out on the outer circle of your radar. You told yourself that you were too busy. You hoped and expected that somebody else would deal with the issue. And you convinced yourself that it wasn't a big deal and that it maybe wasn't a problem, at all.

While you read this, your personal and professional radar will turn on, do a 360-degree sweep, and life's blips will once again appear. You have options. You can

- Immediately shut down the radar and move into complete denial until forced into a panic-stricken reactive mode.

- Tell yourself that you are too busy.

- Wait for someone else to fix the concerns.

- Minimize and deny the existence of the problems.

- Focus energy on the threats and take proactive measures to protect you, your family, and your coworkers from the threat.

The choice is yours. By the way, one of the benefits of keeping your radar turned on is that you will never again be a victim.

Turn on your radar and keep it turned on. Take timely action, as needed.

UNDERSTAND AND HARNESS BSOS (BRIGHT SHINY OBJECT SYNDROME)

IN 2001, I VISITED THE BUDDHIST SHRINE AT SWAYANABATH, located on a hill on the western edge of Kathmandu, Nepal. This Monkey Temple, because it's crawling and leaping with monkeys, is a must-see for anyone visiting this beautiful South Asia entrance to the Himalayas.

Our guide cautioned against getting too close to the monkeys. They bite, she said. She also warned that if we let go of any shiny objects, like cameras, even for a second, the monkeys would snatch and run and do an in-your-face victory dance. They love bright shiny objects.

Monkeys are not the only ones afflicted with bright shiny object syndrome. It afflicts all of us. We are not as rational as we think we are. In fact, we are just a missing link away from being the monkey grabbing the watch. No excuses, just fact.

For years, we have known about the evolutionary process of the brain. We know how in many invertebrates, think worms, the nervous system consists of no more than a net or bundle of nerve cells. After the worms come the goldfish. Next, the bird circling over your head and the croaking frog that keeps you awake at night, also, the snake in the grass that freaks you out. All have well-developed brains made up of the cerebellum, tectum, and basal ganglia. These structures help these creatures see, hear, move about, and respond reflexively (tap on the outside of the goldfish bowl, and you'll know what I'm talking about).

The big leap in evolution came with the development of the outer brain, the neocortex. It is this development, and in particular the frontal region, that is responsible for increased intelligence and the potential for solid executive decision-making.

All mammals have a neocortex, but the higher primates, chimpanzees, and humans have disproportionately larger neocortexes. Not speaking for the chimps, but we humans don't always live up to our potential. We often—way too often—drop down a couple rungs on the evolutionary ladder and lead with the emotion-driven midbrain (think monkeys and bright shiny objects) rather than with our outer rational gray matter.

Why Do Smart People Do Stupid Things?

Question: So why do we smoke, eat too much, drink to excess, watch too much television, not regularly exercise, and fly off the handle at the slightest provocation?

Answer: Because all of these actions, reactions, and nonactions are good for us. Huh? Good for us? Yes, good for us. At least—at a primal level—we feel that way. The monkey brain, which drives BSOS, is automatic, ritualistic, and highly resistant to change. Its only concern is survival, and its only time focus is now. It does not judge behavior or anticipate consequence; it naturally wants pleasure (or freedom from pain) now.

82

The monkey brain is the home of our stress response—the launch point for our decision to fight or take flight. Here, cigarettes are a logical reaction to distress, same for drinking too much. Oversleeping is a logical escape. Drug abuse makes sense, and ditto for many other behaviors that take us out of our conscious world when we perceive the conscious world as a threat. Trace any behavior back far enough, and you will find an emotional payoff. The intent is never to harm oneself. The intent of the monkey is always to feel better regardless what our rational thoughts tell us.

Question: Back up for a second. How do unhealthy behaviors get started in the first place, and why do they continue? From the time we are little, we are all warned about the dangers of tobacco, alcohol, and drugs. We know the benefits of proper nutrition and exercise. What went wrong?

Answer: Now think about it, most unhealthy habits practiced by adults start during their teens and early twenties. Keep in mind the fact that the cerebral cortex and, more specifically, the prefrontal cortex, the home of judgment and reasoning, is the last part of the brain to develop. Most researchers suggest it takes this area of the brain eighteen to twenty years to develop completely—some say as many as twenty-five years.

This slow development means that emotions and emotionally driven behaviors dominate during these years. As an infant, and as a child, our emotions are closely monitored and influenced by our parents and teachers. We are their emotional dependents. However, as we hit the teen years, hormones begin to push the emotional dependency away from the old folks and toward people our age. We seek out and listen to people who look, talk, think, act, and react as we do.

The sage advice, warnings, and demands to stay away from sex, drugs, and rock 'n' roll are increasingly vulnerable to the emotional and visceral pull toward peer acceptance and belonging. No matter what the intellect says. If fighting past coughing, throat burning, and horrible taste is what it takes to smoke cigarettes, then so be it. The same goes for choking down that first beer or fighting off health facts and guilt-strewn lectures about sex and sexual abstinence.

Unfortunately, the more we engage in these behaviors, the more difficult it is to stop them. These new behaviors, with repetition, are pushed to a section of our brain containing the basal ganglia. This area, the prefrontal cortex, is where the neural circuits of long-standing habit are formed and held. The basal ganglia operate without much effort and consume little energy.

What does this mean for behavior? It means that actions that were once unthinkable have become just that—acts done with little or no thought at all. What smoker hasn't lit a cigarette while another one burns in an ashtray? How about pouring a drink while a half-filled glass sits on the table across the room? Biting fingernails without realizing it? Throwing a bag of chips into the shopping cart, automatically? How about that pledge to eat just one?

Habit is the brain remembering, and when behavior brings pleasure, the brain chemistry doesn't want you to forget. Habits form and fight to survive independently of your aspiration to thrive.

CAUTION: MOM, GRAMMA, DAD, GRANDPA. YOU ARE KILLING YOUR KIDS!

OKAY, OKAY, NOT REALLY, BUT GEEZ!

Now that I have your attention, isn't it time we stop feeding our kids so much sugar, salt, and fat? As Grandpa Sam, I know the power of the temptation to give the little ones "treats." They dance for joy and give hugs.

But let's stop for a second and give this some thought. How did this practice get so out of control? Cookies, cakes, and pies aren't new. And they are not going to kill you, not all by themselves, at any rate. We've enjoyed sweets for generations, but past generations didn't have this level of childhood obesity. Past generations didn't have this many overweight kids who become obese, unhealthy adults.

I mean, really, who didn't grow up with a cookie jar? Nobody in my generation, that's for sure! Ours was grayish blue and was in the shape of a teddy bear. I can still see it on the corner of the red-checkered countertop in the pantry. I can still hear the sound of the ceramic lid when I quickly lifted it up and gently (quietly) put it back down.

Rarely was I disappointed. Usually, I grabbed a sugar cookie, a peanut butter cookie, or, best of all, a chocolate chip cookie from the batch that my mom let me help bake.

I close my eyes and hear, smell, and see us now in the kitchen. We take out the bag of sugar, stick of butter, salt, eggs, and flour and go to work. Best part of cooking was when she let me lick the spatula after we scraped out the last bit of dough and put the final cookie on the cookie sheet. Sometimes she let me have a little of the raw cookie dough, not much, just a little. Sometimes she let me have some of the chocolate chips from the brown and orange bag. Of course, she didn't know that I knew where she hid the bag so I would often help myself, just a few. I was always careful to put the rubber band back on just the way she had it.

When it wasn't cookies, it was an apple pie. My dad loved Mom's apple pie. We would always make two. We'd make one for the family and one little one for me. If there was leftover pie crust dough, we would flatten it out with the old wooden rolling pin with green handles, put on lots of butter, sprinkle sugar and cinnamon on top, and put it in the oven until it was nice and crisp. Wow, was that ever good!

Amazing. Those memories come from the early 1950s when I was, oh, I don't know, five or six, maybe. It's now more than sixty years later, and I can still remember little details, including sitting on the counter so I could "help." Boy, I must have really loved those cookies and pies. Or perhaps, it wasn't—or wasn't *just*—the cookies and pies. No, it was much more than just sugar, salt, flour, and fat. It was security. It was love. It was Mom.

On Sunday morning, after church, we would always go over to see Gramma Hayes. She lived on Murray Avenue, the big red house overlooking the old boat-landing on the Chadakoin River. Always a bun in her hair, always with her stockings rolled down to her ankles, always wearing an apron, always with a smile and a ready hug. And always with fresh-baked dinner rolls and cinnamon buns in her bread box or bakery drawer. You could smell the baked goods as soon as you stepped on the porch.

Amazing, how, now, as an aging grandpa, I still remember Sundays at Gramma's. I must have really loved those dinner rolls and cinnamon buns. Or, perhaps, it wasn't—or wasn't *just*—the dinner rolls and cinnamon buns. No, it was much more than just sugar, salt, flour, and fat. It was security. It was love. It was Gramma.

See, the thing is, we didn't know then what we know now. And the food wasn't the same, either. Oh, yes, certainly we've always known about the power of tender moments with those we cherish. We've always known about the strength of love and need to cling to treasured frozen memories. It's the other thing that's kind of new. The fat, sugar, salt thing—the "bad for you" part of the story.

In the 1950s and 1960s, we heard the, "Too much is not good for you" talk and the, "Not until you finish everything on your plate" part, but that was about it. It wasn't until my generation started having kids that the candy-as-boogey-man stories started to appear.

It was around 1972 that the term "junk food" was first used by the Center for Science in the Public Interest. This new "food" is high in salt, fat, and sugar and has lots of preservatives and colorings such as monosodium glutamate and tartrazine and, in some cases, dozens of other things that come from a test tube in a laboratory. Lacking is any real nutritional value that comes with proteins, vitamins, and fiber.

Grocery stores love these foods because they are cheap to produce, have a long shelf life and most of the items require no refrigeration. Bring home a Twinkie and it's just fine for forty-five days without refrigeration! Twinkies are not the only culprit. The same can be said for thousands of other processed foods on the market.

So it begs the question: Is the malnutrition, obesity, heart disease, type II diabetes problem due to Mom's homemade cookies and Gramma's homemade cinnamon buns, or is it the proliferation and convenience of the fast-food industry and the additives used in processed foods? Well, the truth is, both. However, in weighing the harm done to our children and grandchildren (pun intended), the scale not only tips on the side carrying the junk food, it loudly slams on the counter!

Thumbs up to the periodic (not daily) *experience* of Mommy and Granny's homemade goodies served up with an infinite amount of love, kisses, and hugs, and a finite amount of sugar, fats, and salt. And a big, dramatic both thumbs down to anything wrapped in cellophane that stays "fresh" for forty-five days. Oh, sorry, in my book, sugary and diet sodas don't make the grade either. Instead, try, in moderation, fresh-squeezed fruit and serve the kids all the vegetable juice they can swallow.

THE HUMAN PRIMARY OPERATING SYSTEM IS NOT RATIONAL

WE ARE NOT RATIONAL BEINGS WHO EMOTE; WE ARE emotional beings with the capacity to think rationally. Emotion trumps reason. Absent primary prevention, sickness trumps wellness, and survival trumps thrival. It's time for a new social health contract.

Let's be clear. Society (government, healthcare providers, employers) must take the lead role when it comes to responsibility and accountability. However, this is a partnership. A social contract partnership whereby we, the people, voluntarily subjugate the freedom of action we have under the natural state (a state of existence that is not contingent upon man-made laws or beliefs). We do so in order to obtain the benefits provided by the formation of social structures.

Thomas Jefferson and the boys framed our government's responsibility under the umbrella of securing inalienable (natural) rights including life, liberty, and the pursuit of happiness. By obeying man-made laws and complying with accepted standards and mores, we implicitly agree to our part of the social contract. In turn, we have the legal, moral, and ethical ground to demand that the custodians and protectors of our natural rights—our elected officials, medical providers, and employers—be held accountable. This speaks directly to the issue of healthcare access and affordability.

In its simplest form, our implied social health contract requires that society provide

- Awareness of the consequence and benefits of lifestyle choices

- Education needed to initiate and sustain healthy living

- Access to affordable primary, secondary, and tertiary healthcare

- Evidence-based medicine and prevention measures

- Supportive infrastructure (such as parks, healthy worksites, recreational areas, and green space)

And, when provided with all of the above, individuals representing themselves and their minor dependents are responsible for

- Making healthy choices

- Conducting self-exams (paying attention to changes in personal health)

- Completing recommended clinical screenings

- Seeking timely and appropriate medical attention

- Complying with evidence-based recommendations and directives involving lifestyle habits, medications, lab work, and rehabilitation protocols

Accept and respond to the fact that we all fall victim to (and benefit from) evolutionary brain development, biological heredity, and social circumstance. I believe in both free will and determinism. They are not incompatible. There is no tabula rasa, no virgin canvas, or blank piece of paper. I am neither the first nor the sole artist. I do not get to tear off the old sheet and start again fresh and clean.

This gift (and, oh yes, it is a gift) came to me filled with scratches, confusing instructions, perplexing designs, horror, and beauty. I also believe that, independent of my conscious wants and desires, this opportunity—to add my mark—is what I asked for and what I need. My belief is both exhilarating and paralyzing. Either way, it is mine.

If we believe the absence of optimal well-being arises from an individual's free-will choices, the actual biological, social, and economic causes will go unexplored and unaddressed. Resist focusing on lack of willpower or individual blame. Instead, figure out how to limit, constrain, and prevent those situational forces (culture) that propel us toward objectively detrimental lifestyle choices.

Evaluate your contribution to this implied social health contract. Are you advancing the value of awareness, education, access to treatment, evidence-based medicine, evidence-based prevention, and a supportive community culture? If not, why not? And, as an individual, are you keeping up your end of the bargain? If not, why not?

NEVER CROSS A GLACIER WITH A WEAK TEAM

MOUNTAIN CLIMBING AND GLACIER TREKKING REQUIRE superb conditioning and precision teamwork. When tethered on a dangerous slope or when crossing a snow-blown field of ice, your life may depend on who is sharing the rope with you. You must feel confident that, should you slip into a crevasse or lose your balance, your teammates will be able to hold on and pull you to safety. Likewise, you must be able to save someone else and to pull your weight.

Once, when crossing a glacier in Alaska, I was on a line with a young riverboat captain from Juneau who was dogging it all afternoon. Continually, I could feel tension on the line. When I turned around, sure enough, the rope was taut, and I was dragging him up the slope or across the valley.

Considerably older than my riverboat companion and doing my best to drag my own weight, I turned to him after several urgings and warned that the next time I turned around, I would have my Swiss Army blade out and would cut the line. He picked up his pace, and I never had a problem the rest of the day.

FIVE QUESTIONS

1. Would you cross a glacier with your current team?

2. Could you save someone if he or she fell into a crevasse?

3. Would they be able to save you?

4. If necessary, could you use your Swiss Army knife and cut the line?

5. Or, better yet, can you improve your selection and qualifying process to minimize the need to remove members during critical moments of your mission?

If you answered no to any of the questions,
you might wish to consider finding a new team.

WHEN THE GIFT IS REJECTED (MAINTAIN AUTHENTICITY AND CAUTION AGAINST ASSIMILATION)

THE REOCCURRING STORY LINE TELLS THE TALE OF THE youth who awakens one day to the call of adventure. More than an invitation, it is closer in power to a Siren's song—hopefully, without the classic torn sails, broken mast, and floating splinters. Prior to leaving home, our would-be hero's rational thinking plays tug-of-war with his frenetic emotions. In the end, as often is the case, viscera trumps intellect. He goes in search of the grail knowing that, as Joseph Campbell reminds us, there is no security and there are no rules.

On the journey, our hero encounters tests, allies, and enemies. With the aid of a wise mentor—and a writer who knows what Hollywood wants—he conquers all adversity. He captures the flag and sets off back to the village, perhaps even with the once-deadly-but-now-tamed Siren, to share the gift, the prize, the newly found wisdom.

All live happily ever after.

Fade to black…

Okay. Fine. However, there are times when the community rejects the gift, scraps the prize, refutes the newly found wisdom. No matter the treasure, it is still disruptive in the world that knows not, or little, of its existence or value. Truth and authenticity are threatening in a realm of shifting façade. What you may view as the answer may well be seen by others, particularly those in control, as the newest problem to be dealt with, swiftly. When you are the hero, and this happens to you, you have a few options.

- Grab Your Booty and Run (all meanings apply)—Resolve that they are fools not worthy of your treasure. Saddle up for new horizons, confident in the delusion that others elsewhere will readily value what you have to offer.

- Spin and Repurpose the Treasure to Meet the Needs of the Village Elders—With this option, you have tempered your optimism and watered down the strength of your beliefs. You have compromised values, ethics, morals, and sensibilities in exchange for acceptance and security. You have assimilated into an unauthentic system; shame on you.

- Slow Down and Allow Others to Catch Up—Practice Kaizen (continuous improvement, introduced by the Japanese). Without compromise or dilution, break the treasure down into manageable bite-sized pieces and strategically introduce value to those in a position to eventually harvest and distribute the full treasure.

QUANTUM ENTANGLEMENT AND THE POWER OF INTENTION

First, some definitions—

Quantum:

the minimum unit of any physical entity
involved in an interaction

Quantum entanglement:

a quantum physics phenomenon in which the quantum states
of two or more objects have at all times to be described with
reference to each other, each instantaneously tracking changes
to the other, however large the spatial separation of the objects

Intention:

a determination to think and act in a certain way

Elementary physics, my dear, Watson:

- Since the inception (Big Bang), all matter is connected.

- Double slit experiments demonstrate that all matter exhibits properties of both particles and waves—wave-particle duality.

- The mere act of measurement (observation, thought) influences behavior.

Furthermore, the Heisenberg Uncertainty Principle teaches that there can be no circumstance whereby we can describe, with absolute certainty, a particle's definite position and definite momentum.

The more precise we are in measuring a particle's exact location, the more imprecise we are at measuring its destination. And, conversely, as we home in on the momentum, we navigate away from the position. Therefore, the behavior of all physical matter—waves, particles, protons, electrons, and neutrons—is connected, unpredictable, and exists in a pool of infinite potential and possibility.

Got that? Okay, so what?

So what? I'll tell you so what.

It means that we, as card-carrying members of this mostly carbon, hydrogen, oxygen, and nitrogen mass of neutrons, protons, and electrons genus are all related and interdependent. Of course, it also means dung beetles claim kinship but, for today, let's keep the focus on bipeds with highly developed cerebral cortexes.

At a fundamental level, what you do and how you feel matters to me. We are the same. It also means that you, we, are free from the past. The past does not own us. The past does not define who we are. We can change our current direction. Our acceptance or rejection of this fundamental principle of physics—paired with meaningful action—is the key to our present and future well-being.

No small thing, eh?

What are your intentions? Where do you see yourself going? Your thoughts are the gateway to your actions. Focus on the power of the possible and avoid the paralysis of the probable. Yes, life is filled with infinite opportunity, but keep in mind that the door swings both ways. Attitude and action make the difference.

There is nothing either good or bad, but thinking makes it so.

—Shakespeare's *Hamlet*

CAB DRIVERS AND ATTITUDES

Because of travel demands and choices, I take a lot of cabs. I learn a lot about life by asking questions and paying attention. Next time you jump into a taxi, ask the driver for his name. Ask him where he grew up. What state, what town.

If not from the United States, ask him about his homeland. You may learn that he is a highly educated engineer from a poor, underdeveloped nation. His country has no money to hire engineers to build roads, so he's here trying to make enough money to support his wife and kids back home.

Of course, you may find out that your driver is a member of the Hell's Angels. He's driving a cab to save up for a bigger motorcycle. Either way, by showing respectful interest, you'll learn something about a fellow citizen of your planet, something that will probably surprise as well as educate you.

What follows is a snippet from my adventures with cabbies:

Once upon a time, there were three cabbies. They drove the streets of Phoenix, Des Moines, and Minneapolis. Their names were/are/could have been, Chuck from Phoenix, James from Des Moines, and Ivan from Minneapolis. At the time of my cab rides, they each had a completely different outlook on life.

Chuck from Phoenix

Description: Chuck had machine-driven tattoos injected into the back of his neck and the back of his skull. That had to hurt. The design looked like a melted iron cross. He had muscles bulging everywhere except where his belly flowed over his belt like Niagara Falls. Niagara Falls, by the way, is where he roamed the streets as a kid. The truth is, he's from North Tonawanda, but nobody has ever heard of North Tonawanda, so he tells folks he's from Niagara Falls. Everybody knows about Niagara Falls.

His clothes were fine for a weekend of booze, beef, and barbecue, but his overall presentation was not likely to attract return business. Given the conjoined dribbles of sauce resting on the apex of his belly, it's a safe bet that a portion of Kansas City's Best Barbecue slipped off his rack-o-ribs. As for his facial hair, probably left alone for, oh, I don't know, I would guess six days, maybe seven.

Okay, fine. No offensive body odor, no butt crack, and no cigarette smoke. I can handle this.

Now, before I go any further, I want to make it clear that I'm not making a tattoo judgment. My sons have tattoos. The boys, men, are amazing, productive members of society. I love them, dearly. I get it. It's part of the times. I'm old. Who am I to judge? I have a goatee. Hey, I'm just painting a picture.

Attitude: From the moment I get in the cab, he is gruff and ticked off at the world. I know this guy or guys like him. For my first fourteen years, I called western New York home. My guess is he was raised surrounded by coal-blackened snow, grit, grime, gravel pits, and Erie/Lackawanna railroad tracks.

He waved his adolescent defiance flag by having both sides of his hair meet in the back like a duck's butt. In the late 1950s, a spit curl split his forehead. He wore engineer boots and swaggered around with Camel straights rolled up in the sleeve of his T-shirt worn backward, of course. My guess.

He reminded me of Arthur Herbert Fonzarelli, but not as refined, not as polite.

I grew up in Jamestown, New York, in the fifties. Jamestown, the birthplace of Lucille Ball, is about sixty miles from North Tonawanda. As I said, I know the Chucks of the world. From 1956 to 1958, I walked back and forth from Saints Peter and Paul Elementary School. I hid behind shrubs so the Chucks of the world wouldn't see me, chase me, and shake me down for my lunch money.

Chuck's philosophy: Screw 'em. Screw everybody. Get what you can, when you can, while you can. And, along the way, watch out for the Mexicans; they're all drug dealing dopers running from the law like *la cucaracha* from the light. They'd just as soon knife you as look at you. Screw 'em all (HONK, HONK). What airline did you say, buddy? (HONK! HONK! HONK!) @#$%^&*!

My visceral response: Swell. Sigh. Hold on to the lunch money!

James from Des Moines

Description: Standing by the taxi stand at the airport, James struck me as a Chris Farley type without the drugs. Yep, Farley pretty well sums it up. He seemed bigger than most (even for Iowa), affable, and Midwest chic in parka, flannel, hiking boots, winter coveralls, and an Iowa Hawkeye stocking cap.

Attitude: In the middle of a fluffy white snowstorm, James was pleasant with a big smile that matched his big greeting: "Welcome to Iowa, folks!" He said and meant it. I felt it. It was close to midnight, blizzard conditions, and I just arrived from the warm climate and desert beauty of Arizona. Thanks, James! I needed that human warmth in the center of an Iowa freeze.

James's philosophy: Where Chuck's life philosophy was "Screw you! Screw everybody!" James's could best be described by his concerned look: How can I help you? How can I help everybody? There was a long lineup of tired, hungry, wind-blown, frozen people waiting for transportation, and only a few taxis anywhere in the metro area.

When my turn came, the first thing James asked me was, "Sir, would you mind if we take some more of those folks out of the cold and have them share your cab?"

No. I didn't mind at all. I was only sorry and a little ashamed that I didn't think of it myself.

The cab ride to the center of town was jovial, filled with the kind of instant camaraderie that happens to strangers thrown together for short moments in a mini-crisis. James talked about the weather and last year's floods all the while he pledged his allegiance to the flag of the Hawkeye. What could have been a miserable and a freezing end of the day turned out to be just one more reason why I love the state of Iowa and its people. Every time I visit this state, I come away impressed with those who live there. Where do they find all of these genuinely friendly and helpful people?

My visceral response: It's nice to be back in Iowa, and I get to keep my lunch money!

Ivan from Minneapolis

Description: Ivan was dressed more like a limousine driver for an upscale town car service than a shuttle van driver for a hotel chain. I guess fifty-something with a heavy lean toward the something, thinning salt hair with only a hint of pepper. His accent was unmistakably Eastern European. Geography confirmed when he longingly and proudly told me he was from Ukraine.

Attitude: Ivan was upbeat without the sugar and grateful that he had a job. "Thank God, in these days that I have work," he said before the van pulled onto the highway. "I have enough to pay my bills and still send a little money home to my family."

Ivan went on to tell me when he lived in his home country, he was a civil engineer. He lost his job when money dried up, and his department was reduced by more than half.

A relative in Iowa helped him get a civil engineering job in Des Moines. Unfortunately, he was soon laid off. Now he is the 4:00 a.m. to noon shuttle van driver and a part-time employee at a Lowe's home improvement store.

There wasn't a trace of resentment in his voice—only sadness for having to leave his country and gratitude for what America has to offer.

Ivan's philosophy: Work hard, smile, say your prayers, and be grateful for what you have.

My visceral response: Work hard, smile, say your prayers, and be grateful for what you have.

Lessons Learned from My Adventures with Chuck, James, and Ivan

From Chuck, I learned that bitterness and anger feed on a person's character like a pack of desert coyote on an injured mule deer. Chuck's unintended message was that hate and prejudice is far more distasteful than scruffy hair and barbecue stains on a T-shirt. James reinforced the infectious nature and healing properties of kindness and consideration. Ivan? Well, what can I say other than work hard, smile, say your prayers, and be grateful for what you have.

ON THE TRAIL
TO MACHU PICCHU

AFTER SEVERAL HOURS OF TREKKING, THE ROCKY ROAD WAS narrowing, energy was draining, elevation was climbing, and the temperature was dropping.

It was our first camp after leaving Cusco, the ancient capital of Peru. Left behind were the sixteenth-century Spanish cathedrals, little boys selling postcards, weathered old men hoping to shine boots, and pretty little girls selling pretty little dolls. And, also, of course, clean sheets, bottled water, and a warm bed.

Destination: A centennial celebration visit to the ancient ruins of Machu Picchu via the less traveled Salcantay Trail in the magnificent Peruvian Andes.

Jamie, forty-three, our compact Peruvian guide, points toward the heavens, toward the south celestial pole. "Miguel, look up. There! You see? That's the Southern Cross. Do you see the four points of the cross?"

The southern sky ushers deep personal, imaginative, emotional honesty. Jamie's encouragement to look up is spoken to a slightly stooped, quietly aging, snowcapped mountaineer with failing eyes and knees; however, he is heard by a wide-eyed little boy transfixed and energized once again by the wonder of it all.

How could I see anything other than a dense, glorious blanket of shimmer and sparkle? In a time-travel flash, I'm looking at a night sky from my distant past. The sky I remember from summer nights at Lake Erie. Quick glimpses of the time when the Yankees owned their cross-town rivals. A moment in time when thoughts about my heart throb in second grade, Suzie Whitmore, caused joy, stirrings, confusion, and other things that I couldn't share with Sister Mary Louise.

Of course, it wasn't at all like a July, Lake Erie night in the 1950s. The few times I've been south of 22° N latitude, Jamie wasn't helping me interpret the southern skies. Before that night on the snowy and rugged Salcantay Trail to Machu Picchu, I had never seen the beauty of the Crux. Nor had I even imagined other southern deep-sky splendors such as the Coal Sack, the Jewel Box, the Eta Carinae Nebula, the Wishing Well Cluster, the Southern Pleiades, Alpha Centauri, or Omega Centauri.

"Yes, yes, I do see it! It's magnificent!" the star-struck boy said to the affable guide. I forgot how truly beautiful the stars can be. Look at the Milky Way! Now, what is that and that bright one just above the horizon and those three stars pointing west? Are they part of a constellation as well?

Who needs Suzie Whitmore, or even the Yankees, when night treasures like these can be yours just by opening your eyes and looking up with a child's endless wonder?

Over the next several days, Jamie Vasquez and our American guide from International Mountain Guides, Kelly Ryan, would go on to guide us safely through the Salcantay Pass. They led us along dangerous narrow ledges in the high Amazon cloud forest, up and down rugged mountain trails, over rickety bridges, and on into the ancient ruins of Machu Picchu.

Ever the teacher, Jamie enlightened and entertained us with running narratives. He spoke of Inca history, local customs, sacred mountains, coca leaves, chicken calls, and the proper way to eat passion fruit. He shared Andes myths and legends. We learned about native flora and fauna, conquistadors, Emperor Pachacuti, Hiram Bingham, the secrets of ancient stone architecture, and a new way to think about orchids.

When asked, Why do you climb? The Italian mountaineer Giusto Gervasutti responded:

> We have many forms of mountaineering. It may take the form of a need to live heroically, or to rebel against restraint and limitation: an escape from the restricting circle of daily life, a protest against being submerged in universal drabness, an affirmation of the freedom of the spirit in dangerous and splendid adventure. It may be the search for an intense aesthetic experience, for exquisite sensations, or for man's never satisfied desire for unknown country to explore, new paths to make. Best of all, it should be all these things together.

Yes, all that he said, and more. Often I am asked, Why? Why do I do this? This meaning moving out of a predictable and defined comfort zone and heading smack-dab into the path of guaranteed discomfort and potentially life-threatening danger.

Well, if you haven't walked a mile in these moccasins or stumbled a kilometer in these boots, no answer I give will make sense. However, if you get the boots part, you won't feel the need to ask the question. Also, my guess is that we have shared moccasin trails somewhere along the journey. That said, besides the beauty and adventure, it's about sharing life's path with my brothers and sisters.

Teachers and Lessons

Jamie was not the only teacher on this pilgrimage. In the course of my sixty-six years, I have learned the importance of paying attention to my fellow travelers, of learning from their words and—more importantly—their actions and intentions.

With a bow to Chaucer, let me introduce you to my adventure companions and the well-being life lessons they taught as we trekked to Machu Picchu. By the way, we all have forever-memory friends who have taught us wonderful life lessons. I encourage you to sketch short profiles of your fellow or sister pilgrims, similar to those presented now.

Doyle: So how exactly do you wrap a 130-word description around a man as big as Doyle? He is physically big, sure; north of both six feet and two-hundred pounds—Seattle Seahawks tight-end big, but with a heart and soul much greater than that.

Loose gravel, ahead, Mike, be careful. Narrow at the bend, keep to your left. How's your knee holding out? Do you need more blister pads? Throughout the journey, Doyle always had a smile and always conveyed a genuine sense that, should you need anything, he'd be the first to help. His pleasant disposition and Good Samaritan manner were spontaneous, an automatic, natural way that comes from what?

- A simple, small-town Texas upbringing?
- A beautiful life partner?
- Nurtured and trusted friends?
- Innate sensibilities?
- Lessons learned from the athletic field?
- Intentionally cultivated core values?
- Experience as a dad and grandfather?
- The luck of the draw?
- The sum impact of years of living, discerning, teaching, learning, frustration, joy, disappointment, success, failure, discipline, sharing, and loving?

Yes. I'm going with all of the above.

Judie: Wow. Where do I begin? I'll just put fingers on the keyboard and see where this goes.

Woman: Determination is thy name. Judie is solidly anchored at the intersection where tenacity meets steel. She presents the most potent blend of drive, sense of purpose, indomitable spirit, and intellectual curiosity that I have ever encountered on any mountain trail. At one point, a badly jammed big toe forced her to take the short train ride from Vilcanota (the hydroelectric station) to Aguas Calientes (Machu Picchu Pueblo). She sat looking out the window, simmering to a slow boil. She was not pleased to watch the scenery from a cozy railroad car while her companions walked the two-hour path on the tracks.

Well, not all of her companions walked. One other trekker, who would be me, also rode the train. Judie, while forever pleasant, was clearly disappointed. Intellectually, she understood the need to avoid further damage to her toe, but emotionally she didn't want to miss a single footfall on the trail to Machu Picchu. As for me, I gleefully welcomed the opportunity to take the train and rest my aching knees.

During this period of time, Judie was a veteran marathon runner, cyclist, disciplined fitness aficionado, and overall ferocious consumer of all that life has to offer. She was not in the habit of truncating challenge nor did she let a black toe hold her back for long.

Once we arrived at Machu Picchu, she was at the front of the pack, hiking the steep steps, traveling the narrow trail to the ancient drawbridge, and testing Jamie's recall of all things Inca. Of course, I felt the obligation to drag along at the back—in case anyone was tempted to move too fast.

Oh, did I forget to mention that Judie is Doyle's wife and she, too, is seventy? Yep, seventy, looking forty and traveling the trails like a kid on spring break. Some couples may choose to celebrate milestone events like a fiftieth wedding anniversary by sitting at the seashore sipping fruity cocktails in the evening and taking slow beach walks in the morning. Not Doyle and Judie. They chose instead to mark their five decades by trekking rugged mountain switchbacks, musing life's mysteries in a tent under the Southern Cross, and retracing the steps of ancient Inca emperors.

Wow, indeed!

John: On every mountain expedition, there are rabbits, and there are turtles. Some dressed better than others. John was one dapper bunny!

There were times when I couldn't tell if the dust plume was caused by the mules and horses heading back to their corrals, or by John racing on ahead like a young colt feeling his oats. High energy, enthusiastic, attentive, friendly, and uncomplaining are just some of the ways to describe John.

He was also fully into the culture, sporting Andes fashion with the flair of an ancient Inca prince. Hat, sweater, ring, pants, and colorful tote transformed John from just another foreign trekker into a walking advertisement for festive Peru. And, fortunately, he displayed an excellent sense of humor.

At sixty-seven, John was added to my growing list of role models. His zest for life, sharp mind, and eclectic interests advance his quality of life while enhancing the experience of all of us who traveled with him. Of course, it was clear that his life partner, Linda, was his spark.

Linda: Well, the cliché about the broken record is becoming increasingly apparent. Like Judie, dignified, gentle, energetic, and intelligent best describes Linda. So do the words funky, spunky, and spirited. Linda showed great compassion as well. Naturally concerned about her two-legged companions, but she was very interested and attentive to the growing problem of stray dogs that take to the Peruvian streets, landfills, and trails.

Don't feed stray dogs! Don't feed stray dogs? Yeah, right. You tell her, not me.

As for her fitness, I was struck by how fluid and efficiently she moved. Like her dear friend Judie, Linda is an elite athlete with over thirty marathons entered and completed. Again, while other folks past the age of sixty are checking the Gray Line tour schedule, Linda and John are planning their next mountain expedition. Perhaps their next adventure will include watching the sunrise from the summit of Mount Kilimanjaro. Or, perhaps, visiting the sacred Buddhist monastery in Tengboche while trekking to the Mount Everest base camp in Nepal. Rest assured that no moss will grow under their boots, and no dust will cling to their hiking sticks.

Ian: Ian is a gentle, burly mountaineer of Scottish heritage who wears kilts, but, no, not on the trail—chafing, you know. Duh. And when it's cold, he covers his shaved dome with *Where the Wild Things Are* headgear. Yep, that's Ian. And, of course, it's not all that Ian is, but it does paint an interesting picture, no?

Boy, here's a guy I'd like to know better. Ian is a talented photographer and an excellent team member with a sense of independence that neither looks for nor appears to need your permission. That's not to suggest defiance or lone wolf countenance in any way, more like quiet self-assurance—the kind that neither judges nor asks for judgment. You get the sense that with Ian, there are no games, no façade, no hype, no posturing or guesswork. I got the impression that an old soul was wearing those kilts, an old soul who had worn through more than one pair of boots and indeed many pairs of brogues along his journey.

Good guy. I'd gladly share another dusty road with Ian and another Pisco Sour too. Now, would I share a heaping, steaming plate of haggis with him? Probably not. You're on your own with that one, Scotty!

Rodica: Roady was a delightful travel companion in every way.

I didn't have an opportunity to speak with Roady nearly as much as I wish I had (another rabbit to this turtle). She always had a smile and an encouraging word for others as she quietly buried herself in the wonders of the trip. She and Ian, engaged, were young enough to be the children of the rest of us. However, they never made us senior folks feel as if we were slowing them down.

I enjoyed the bookend feature of Doyle and Judie's rearview mirror reflections and Ian and Rodica's private, silent—but clearly evident—tender foreshadowing of a wonderful life of love and adventure to come.

Well-Being Life Lessons Learned
along the Trail to Machu Picchu

- Don't just look at your books, look up.

- Prepare for and live a life of healthy uncertainty.

- Care of others is the purest form of self-love.

- Patience with one impacts success for all.

- Humor clears the head and energizes the body.

- Be aware of and beware of the chronologically superior.

- Age is just a number.

- Better to be slow and safe than fast and reckless.

- Expect the best and prepare for the worst.

- Kindness knows no boundaries.

- Personal passion plus team support equals success.

- Vet leadership carefully and then follow instructions.

- Enjoy the journey. In the end, that's all there is.

- Embrace the power of the possible.

SITUATIONAL WELLNESS: LESSONS FROM THE *BALTIMORE CATECHISM*

Do you practice situational wellness? No judgment, just a question without bias, implied value, or finger wagging. Who am I to judge?

The question may also be rhetorical because we all practice situational wellness. You know, wellness when it suits our needs and doesn't interfere with our momentary whims. While I'd like to think we have control over our every-moment behavior, we don't. That fact is very evident. Just look around, better yet, think about your behavior. It's part of our nature to give in periodically to monkey brain and BSOS (bright shiny object syndrome). It's a feature of our evolution. This is an important acknowledgment and admission. Enlightenment and Buddha sightings are rare where I come from and, my guess, where you live as well.

Join with me and repeat, *Unlike the Buddha, I practice situational wellness.*

This fact does not mean that we are weak, corrupt, or inadequate. Lacking enlightenment does not mean that we are evil or the anti-Buddha. It means that we are human. It means that we are imperfect. I encourage you to embrace and celebrate your imperfection and that of others. To do otherwise is to live a life of self-recrimination, denial, stress, shame, guilt, contradiction, and duplicity.

Before I go further, let me give you my definition of wellness. I've presented this before, but it's important for this context.

> *Wellness: a dynamic, objective and subjective progression toward a state of complete physical, intellectual, emotional, spiritual, and social well-being and not merely the absence of disease or infirmity. Incremental improvements can occur from preconception up to and including a person's last breath.*

For the purpose of this essay, the key root words are dynamic, progress, and increment. With wellness, there is no end point, at least not in this lifetime. Wellness is a paradoxical state in which contentment of being and aspiration of becoming live in harmony.

As a result, it is not the independent act or goal that is the concern. It is the understanding and intention (moral and ethical integrity) that separates the saint from the sinner. Once again, it's all about context.

1955, Sister Mary Wilma and the Baltimore Catechism

Bear with me as I take us back to the year 1955, Saints Peter & Paul School on Cherry Street in Jamestown, New York. Dogwood is in bloom, forsythia paint the backyard a bright yellow, my First Holy Communion is fast approaching (nifty white suit), and I have just reached the Age of Reason.

Receiving First Holy Communion means that I am now morally responsible for my sins. Hell could be my fate—will be my fate—unless and until I understand, embrace, and follow the teachings of the *Baltimore Catechism.*

When I was seven, I was barely able to remember my phone number yet alone all those rules and regulations. However, that said, all these years later, I find some splendid guidelines posted in that little blue book. Whatever your religious or philosophical equivalent may be, it's worth retrieving the moral teachings of your youth and seeing how they might apply to your world today.

What Would the Baltimore Catechism *Say about Wellness?*

Loosely interpreted, lesson six in the BC defines the existence of sin in terms of right or wrong, awareness and willful action. Something has to be indeed wrong, you must know it's wrong, and you must do it anyway. When these three criteria are met, you've sinned. There's also an order of seriousness of sin based on how much damage it does to your soul. The grievance can be material (didn't know), venial (small), or mortal (humongous). Again, this is a loose interpretation.

So in the world of wellness, you know you're a sinner if

- There is evidence that the behavior you're considering is, in any way, physically, emotionally, or spiritually harmful to yourself or others.

- You are well aware of the harm the behavior will cause.

- You do it anyway.

Going back to the context, if your intention is to do something you know to be harmful, you've compromised your integrity for the perceived reward or the expediency of the moment. It is this latter part, for the moment, that makes all of us practitioners of situational wellness.

My message is not to preach: STOP DOING IT! In many cases, that would be both naïve and hypocritical on my part. To quote Pope Francis, "Who am I to judge?" Unless you have achieved enlightenment, odds are, to some degree, you're going to continue it and so am I. The issue is to make sure you're not in denial about harm, and to be careful when it comes to measuring the strength of your sins.

Eat all the birthday cake you want, drink all the booze on Friday nights you choose, eat those occasional cheeseburgers to your heart's content (or discontent). Feel free to give children pop, fat, and processed sugar, and call it a treat. Smoke that celebratory cigar but just don't tell yourself that you're not an active and informed member of the SW (situational wellness) family. You are both active and, in this case, enlightened. Accept the responsibility and the consequences.

If, according to known science, something is harmful, all the spinning in the world won't change the evidence. Eating and serving jelly-filled donuts may be a venial sin compared to the mortal sin of deep-fried Snickers. However, they are both filled with known toxins. If the intent is to stay on a path of wellness, you should, at the very least, acknowledge the science and, at best, avoid the behavior.

No judgment—I'm sure you'll still go to heaven. I'm just asking for honesty, responsibility, and accountability. That's all. Oh, and be careful about using the this-may-be-bad-for-my-body-but-every-once-in-a-while-it's-good-for-my-spirit! line. As you well know, this is a slippery slope. Besides, 99 percent of the time, *this* can be replaced by something that won't cause harm.

Avoiding the Near Occasion of Sin

I also can hear the good Sister talk about the importance of having a firm purpose of sinning no more and to avoid near occasions of sin. By near occasions of sin, BC means all the persons, places, and things that may easily lead us into temptation. Something about He who loves the danger will perish in it.

The four kinds of occasions are these:

- Near occasions, through which we always fall
- Remote occasions, through which we sometimes fall
- Voluntary occasions, or those we can avoid
- Involuntary occasions, or those we cannot avoid

Well, like I said, you and I, we're going to sin. That's a fact. The question is: Are you serious about avoiding unhealthy habits and actions—those you know to be harmful? Or, for you, is there no paradox at all? Doth thou protest too much about Being with only minor action toward Becoming? This fundamental question is important for you to figure out and answer, honestly. No judgment, just a nudge toward self-awareness and honesty.

Meanwhile, those donuts sure look good, right? Ah, what the heck, one can't hurt, right?

Let me suggest a personal mission statement for every SW practitioner (all of us) to consider: My personal mission is to progressively and consistently achieve measurably higher levels of physical, emotional, intellectual, and spiritual awareness by living a life of integrity, curiosity, authenticity, compassion, and dedication to the collective needs of all beings.

An Ongoing Argument for Creating Healthy Cultures

Even if you adopt this personal mission statement as your own, it's not good enough. We need help. We need the help of the community to protect the health of the individual. I hope it's clear by now that we are not good at self-monitoring; this is not pejorative, just good old observation sprinkled with brain science.

Rational thought plays second fiddle to knee-jerk, emotional reaction. Schools, worksites, government, and family structure must provide safe, secure environments that foster wellness (as defined here) while helping individuals avoid the near occasion of sin.

And, yes, this means no donuts at conferences, no sugar treats at school functions, and no candy bowls on desks. Also, no deep-fried Twinkies, pickles, ice cream, brisket, Philly cheesesteaks, or Snickers on a stick at the state fair!

Yes, you read that paragraph correctly. Trust me, you will more than survive, you will *thrive*!

DON'T CONFUSE CONNECTIVITY WITH INTIMACY

Stop for a second and consider the possibility that the more touch-points we have, the less in touch we've become.

The other day, I heard a TV reporter ask a twenty-something woman how often she talked on the phone. Her response was, almost never. She, like most of those under forty, prefers texting to actual phone calling. Her response as to why she texts: I find that texting allows me to avoid the awkwardness that comes with actual interaction.

No, seriously, that's what she said. As for the reporter, not an eyebrow raised or a follow-up question asked.

Is it just my thinning white hair that finds "allows me to avoid the awkwardness that comes with actual interaction" alarming, or are there others of you out there who are more than a little troubled by her answer? Yes, I understand the value of texting and instant messaging, and I realize that the sheer numbers of contacts and connections has increased significantly. This part is all fine. The creepy part is that, knowingly or not, I think she nailed a reality. Have we, indeed, exchanged intimacy and actual interaction for expediency and ease?

As for the full-spectrum world of technology, it's been said that computers like IBM's Watson will never entirely replace humans. Robots cannot convey the subtlety and nuance often used to deliver the actual meaning behind our messages. All of us have dozens of shades of smiles, frowns, voice inflections, intonations, body postures, eye shifts, eyebrow lifts, and squints that add color, texture, and clarity to our interactions.

As a university professor, lecturer, mentor, and trainer of hundreds of health promotion professionals, I always stress the importance of crystal-clear communication. The order of preference for personal communication is

- Actual face-to-face

- Electronic face-to-face (Facetime, Skype)

- Audio (formally known as telephone)

- Video message

- Audio message

- Descriptive personal e-mail

- Text message

Wait, before anyone calls me old or out of touch, let me again praise technology and its value in disease prevention, health promotion, and daily living, in general. I love it for peer support, reminders, data transfer, medical monitoring, rallying action, spreading information, quick hellos, and growing social networks. It truly is remarkable, and we've just scratched the surface. Hot damn, hallelujah, and bring it on. My kids get the best hand-me-downs you can imagine.

Please, please, please, along with high-tech, keep fostering and building high touch. A few years back, I thoroughly enjoyed watching the IBM computer kick butt on *Jeopardy!* but it's hard to imagine *Dinner with Watson* coming to a theater near you. Also, all the emoticons in the world can't replace a hug, a knowing look, or an actual smiley face from a real little kid. I don't find interactions with them awkward at all.

HOWARD BEALE ISN'T THE CRAZY ONE AND MR. SPOCK IS DANGEROUS

You know Howard. He's the "I'm not going to take this anymore" guy. Howard is the oh-so-angry, fictitious news commentator from Paddy Chayefsky's award-winning movie, *Network* (1976).

> *I want you to get up right now. Sit up, go to your windows, open them and stick your head out and yell, "I'm as mad as hell and I'm not going to take this anymore!" Things have got to change! Friends; you've got to get mad! Then, we'll figure out what to do about the depression and inflation and the oil crisis… First, get out of your chairs, sit up out of your chair, go to your window, stick your head out, say it: "I'm mad as hell and I'm not going to take it anymore!"*

You go, Howard! Tell it like it is!

Next year, 2016, marks the fortieth anniversary of *Network*. Coincidentally this is also my fortieth year as a health and wellness professional. It's amazing (somewhat disheartening) that—other than objects of distraction—Paddy could have tapped out those words this morning.

Those of you who know my work know that I view the process of change as a linear, sequential process. The stages are intellectual (information), emotional (engagement), visceral (call to action), and cellular (habit formation). The key stage is the visceral stage. Or, as Howard would say, the "I'm mad as hell, and I'm not going to take it anymore!" stage.

Sustainable change does not occur until your soul awakens, and your bones start shakin'.

During all of my years in the field of public health and health policy, I've seen tons of data and periodic bursts of emotion but precious little soul-awakening, bone-shaking action. As for sustained change—please—don't make me go get Howard. He's still ticked.

The question is why. Why do we not see, feel, and believe that the health platform is truly burning? Why can't we hear the crackle? Why can't we smell the acrid smoke? Is Howard right? Do you really think this (the health of our nation, our children) is the way it's supposed to be? Is it time for you to get up, go to your windows, stick your head out and yell?

Things have got to change.

Mr. Spock Is Dangerous

I just participated in my umpteenth health promotion conference; many of the same faces, many of the same tiresome PowerPoint slides. More studies are coming soon. Yes, Yes, YES! Research is critical, but it's time to shift more of the science of life research to art-of-living research. Facts without texture and context are meaningless.

Until we can answer the corporate and personal *so what?* question, *the why should I care?* question, we will remain trapped in this endless cycle of information and transient emotion. Until we objectively tee-up the aha moment that subjectively awakens souls and shakes bones, we are in danger of doing more harm than good.

We don't need any more tinder. We need sparks!

Excuse me. I have to stop now. It's time for Howard and me to get some fresh air.

WITHOUT AN IRRITANT, THERE CAN BE NO PEARL

BE HONEST. IT'S MUCH EASIER—AND SAFER—TO SIT BACK, complain, and wait for the dedicated others to take action than it is to do something.

For many of us, spectator is the chosen role, unless and until there is a defined passion, steely commitment, and laser-focus determination to get involved and advance change. When these three driving forces are present, our bones shake and our spirits soar. We can't sit still, we can't wait for someone else, and we can't shut up. We stir and spit, shout and stomp our feet. We seize and run with the torch. We become Emperor Napoleon Bonaparte I. We don't need the Pope. We can crown ourselves! Time is fleeting. Daylight is burning. There are causes to advance and worlds to conquer.

This seems particularly the case for cancer thrivers or anyone who has conquered serious physical, psychological, or social challenges. The old adage, "That which does not kill us makes us stronger," attributed to Friedrich Nietzsche, is true.

In my book, *Voices from the Edge*, I present the wisdom of real people who have been diagnosed with and treated for cancer. I tell the survival stories of ten individuals who faced death, who walked to the edge and returned. These individuals and thousands more who have met death face-to-face and won the stare down gain new vision, a new love for life in its most brilliant and enchanting detail. They experience clearly its music and colors and scents and wonders, the daily miracles that were always there, but which, like most of us, they previously took for granted.

Often these individuals choose to carry the banner on social issues concerning health awareness, children's health, and community health policy. Do not tell these folks what they cannot do. If what they seek is within the realm of possibility, they will stare you down every time.

Is the title of Emperor too much? Okay. How about CI? Chief Irritant. You can be the sand that produces the nacre, the saliva-like substance that hardens to become a pearl. So let someone else sit back and complain. Let the masses stay in the bleachers because just below the surface are pearls in-waiting, and you are the irritant, the catalyst that can make it all happen.

Let the spitting begin!

Caution: Sophocles was right. No one loves the messenger who brings bad news. As I have stated before, there are times when the elders reject the wisdom you offer. Knowledge and innovation are disruptive in the world that does not value change. Proposed solutions may be viewed by others, particularly those in control, as an attack on their leadership and a threat to their power and status.

It's no fun when people spit at you. Trust me. I've been there. While being a Chief Irritant is not always sunny and rain free, I like to think that, along the way, I've triggered the start of a few pearls. For the most part, I've dodged the spray, toweled off, and lived to irritate again.

Ten Ways to Survive and Thrive as a Community Chief Irritant

1. Fasten your armor (it's going to be a bumpy night).

2. Pursue your need for popularity elsewhere.

3. Find a powerful champion to support you and advance your cause.

4. Practice no-oblique-speak.

5. Compromise on tactics—not ethics or integrity.

6. Irritate without judgment or arrogance.

7. Beware the ides of March (*et tu*_____).

8. Establish a no-jerks-allowed rule and embrace the spirituality of imperfection.

9. If you think everyone around you is a jerk, look in the mirror.

10. Repeat after me: spit is good!

WARNING: ASSIMILATION DEAD AHEAD!

Assimilate:
to absorb into the culture or
mores of a population or group

Have you ever experienced a situation, group, or culture that you initially considered (sensed or thought) was wrong, odd, or dangerous? In a matter of months, did you identify that same situation, group, or culture as normal and desirable?

Yes? Caution: You have assimilated.

What started out as dangerous, confusing, and belly-wrong—opposite of any logic you've ever encountered—morphed into the norm, your new standard. What was that? What happened? While this may be a good thing, it may also signal that you have compromised values, ethics, morals, and sensibilities in exchange for acceptance and security.

You need to be careful that you don't lower your standards and go against your better judgment in the face of financial, social, or organizational pressure. Be careful of just-this-one-time thinking and avoid practicing situational ethics, a horribly abused and misunderstood theory of ethics.

- Under what circumstances are physical and emotional abuses acceptable?

- Since when are failing grades not a big deal?

- Why is lying to your mom wrong but lying to the IRS okay?

- When did it become accepted practice that a kid who smokes dope several times a week is just experiencing a life passage and practicing a recreational activity instead of engaging in an addictive and illegal behavior?

- How is it that sugary soda is bad for your child's health but good as a fundraiser for his school?

- Why is it that your kid being obese is fine with you because she's not as big as the other children?

- When did unethical behavior, such as Lance Armstrong cheating in cycling and baseball players using steroids, become okay and "just the way it is?"

The list goes on and on.

Before taking any action that you may regret, pay attention to all of your senses and listen to your internal voice. You know what I'm talking about—the gut whisper that says slow down, danger ahead. Tune into that mild panic sensation that tells you that you are about to swim outside the roped area.

SPIRITUALITY: OPEN YOUR EYES, IT'S ALL AROUND YOU

Forever present without need of definition
Invisible to some, blindingly radiant to others
Existing without beckon
Eternally ours

WHEN HE WAS TWENTY, I TOOK OUR SON DEREK ON A TRIP to Arizona. Our stops included tourist mainstays—the Grand Canyon, Sedona, Meteor Crater, ancient Native American ruins, the Petrified Forest, and a side trip to Monument Valley up on the Utah border. Experienced before and, as with so many things, experienced for the first time.

For some, a trip like this begs for a concise, flat, colorless summary. Something like this:

A big hole in the ground with lots of funny-looking rocks along a very steep and winding road. Another hole in the ground caused by a big rock that fell out of the sky. Cactus-covered rocks. Rock from where there used to be wood. Finally, at the end of a long drive, dust and more strange-looking rocks.

There's nothing wrong with this description; quite frankly, it's accurate.

Fortunately, that is not the trip I experienced with my son.

On our trip to the Grand Canyon, the ancient, friendly, innocent Anasazi people showed us how to make split-twig figures; Major John Wesley Powell, fresh from the horror of the American Civil War, took us on a roller-coaster ride down the Colorado River on a wooden raft; and we stood behind Timothy O'Sullivan as he ducked under the hood of his camera to take the first photographs of a view that cannot be captured or held with an artificial lens or stored on a photo-magnetic plate.

For some, the hike we took to the floor of the canyon could best be described as long, exhausting, icy, dangerous, cold, hot, wet, and dusty times two. The only tangible result came in the form of half-dollar-sized blisters.

Fortunately, that was not our hike.

For us, scenes changed with every turn. Colors melted together, then quickly, magically, formed distinct boundaries. Squirrels led the way, and large black birds seemed to wish us well—or perhaps they were just teasing us along a trail marked with the footprints of four seasons.

When my son asked, "How you doing, old man?" some conservative souls might have raised an eyebrow at the apparent disrespect. I, on the other hand, delighted in the display of comfort, friendship, father-son love, and intimacy.

For still others, the car we sat in for eleven hundred miles over three days would be a slow-moving prison lacking only a dead albatross. They would complain about the cramped lodging and tasteless food. Looking out the car window, they only see an endless ribbon of desert sage and red dirt.

Fortunately, that was not the road we traveled.

Our road had frequent stops to record images that would later trigger crystalline memories. We shared moments of companionship with total strangers. We saw wondrous sights that brought more questions than either of us had answers. Best of all, our road spilled secrets, reflections, fears, regrets, joys, hopes, and dreams too often reserved for midday talks by gray beards on green park benches.

We know, of course, that the roads, the rocks, and the rivers in our lives exist independently of us. However, the beauty, the mystery, the inspiration, and the fellowship they spark help us to be truly conscious in their presence. If we are not, they remain only rocks, roads, and rivers.

Years ago, after giving a speech to local civic leaders at Brooklyn College, I was approached by a woman from the audience, a distinguished-looking Caribbean woman. She sensed, she said, that I was a very spiritual person. She wondered what was the physical source of my spiritual nature. With an intuitive tilt of her head and a questioning furrow in her brow, she leaned forward and asked, "Was it your mother?"

The quick answer was and is yes.

In the face of many challenges, my mother always saw past problems and focused on the promise and beauty of life. She endured my father's alcoholism. She nursed his decade of disability, his cancer, and his death at the age of sixty-seven. Mother was optimistic and hopeful. However, she worried and agonized over the sad life and early death of my sister who died at the age of thirty-three. In her seventies, mother Mary accepted her lingering affliction with emphysema and the toll it took on her heart.

Some people would see her life as difficult, filled with disappointment and worry. Others would feel sorry for her and wonder how she got through the days. Some would pray for her as they counted their blessings. They would view the cards she held, shake their heads, and thank God they did not have to suffer those years.

Fortunately, the life they saw was not the life she lived.

Yes, of course she felt pain and heartache, but for every dark moment, she lived a thousand love-filled hours. For every misfortune, she saw a hundred reasons to rejoice in the treasures of life. For every physical pain, she found countless moments of bliss. For every fear she experienced today, she knew the promise of tomorrow.

Toward the end of her life, she needed the full-time attention of a nursing home. I remember visiting with her one cold, rainy day in March 1995, a few months after she settled in. I came into her room and saw her, lying on her side, shriveled from osteoporosis, still lovely at the age of eighty-three.

Recently awakened from her nap, she smiled at me and said, "My cup runneth over. I am the luckiest person alive. I have good people to take care of me, a comfortable place to live, and friends and family who love me."

She meant every word. Broken and bleeding paper-thin skin, multiple fractures, emphysema, living in a nursing home—and she believed she was the luckiest person on earth! Positive. This was the way she lived, one of the many lessons she quietly taught.

My brothers and I called her every day, usually in the evening, to see how she was feeling. One day I called about midmorning. She wanted to know why I was calling. I reminded her that I spoke with her just about every day. She said, yes, but why now? I explained that I would be away during the early evening hours and wanted to make sure I spoke with her today. She seemed curiously concerned that I had called when I did. She said she was tired and wanted to rest. Would I please call her tomorrow? As always, we said, I love you, then goodbye.

That was our last goodbye.

Later that evening a cousin, who visited mother every night, called to say that my mom died peacefully at seven that night—about the time I usually called. My heart broke. I told my wife and our three children. We held each other and cried. Later that night, I sat in a hot tub and howled at the moon till I could only whimper like a lost pup.

Three young women, attendants from the nursing home, came to the funeral, something they usually did not do. They wanted to tell me what happened after I last spoke with my mother. They said she took a nap, and when she awoke, she smiled at them and said that she was going to die later that day. They had never heard her speak like this—what they perceived to be as negative.

They all said, "Mary, you're fine, you are not going to die."

She said, yes, she was, but it was okay. Earlier that day, she told them she had seen my father, nineteen years deceased; my sister, twenty-one years passed; and her mother, twenty-eight years gone. They had come to her, held out their hands, and said it was time.

The young women said my mother was at peace as she told them this.

May we all live such a life, and may we all pass with such dignity and peace.

TREASURE, RESPECT, AND NURTURE YOUR SPIRITUAL NATURE

SPIRITUALITY IS THE FRAGILE WRAPPING THAT HOLDS everything together, so evanescent, and yet so tightly clinging that we can barely distinguish where it ends and where we begin. Light passes through, but only those who open their eyes and let it penetrate can see what's really there. And know that, more than simply clinging tightly, the spiritual universe is part of us all and we are part of it—that we are truly one.

With this knowledge comes the key that opens the door to beauty, mystery, inspiration, and an actual physical sense of being part of the spiritual whole. Of course, we must pick up the key and use it. Too often, we look at it with both longing and fear, hesitant to unlock the door and peek around the corner, wanting the treasures but afraid of the risks. Content with the knowledge that it is there, we say, Someday. We say, Maybe—but no, not today, and no promises.

Unfortunately, many others go about their lives totally ignorant of the spirit's presence or its force. Or if they choose to acknowledge a spiritual power, they do so passively, often as a victim: *Why did God do this to me?* The world is a cold, cruel place. *Why can't I get a break?* I never have any luck.

To these people, the realm of the spirit is mysterious, perhaps mythical. It is separate and apart from their world, which is a universe of indifference at best and cruel intention at worst. They are merely pawns, at the mercy of unknown and unseen forces. Their lives are spent hiding from imaginary evils or running from real demons of their creation.

I am a spiritual person, but not what most would call religious. I do not follow one strict dogma, nor do I worship within the confines of bricks and mortar. However, I firmly believe in the power and glory of forces that I do not understand. I believe in a God that was forever before and will be forever after. I believe that the energy called Michael will continue after my flesh is dust. I believe that I will share conscious space and energy with my mother, my father, my sister, my brother, my granddaughter, and all who have left this physical world.

We rightfully pay a price for deliberately continuing to act in ways that hurt others—a consequence that transcends physical boundaries. I am governed and buoyed by these beliefs, and I carry them not just for comfort and protection but also because of a sincere commitment to their independent existence.

MARRIAGE AND PARTNERSHIPS: ASSESSING RISK

RELATIONSHIPS CAN BE FLAGGED ACCORDING TO RISK ranging from those with a high likelihood of splitting up to those with minimal risks. While certainly no ironclad guide, here's a look at the various types of marriages and partnerships in descending order of risk.

1. **I Don't Want to Talk About It.** *Neither Do I.*

   Pure denial. Both individuals live in the world of make-believe, the world where discomfort equates to failure, where discovery beckons disaster. Best not talk about it for fear it is—or will become—real.

   Prognosis: Don't bother to freeze the ceremonial cake. Nobody will be around for the thaw.

2. **Let's Talk.** *I Don't Want To.*

   Usually with this couple, it is the wife who wants to talk and confront problems head on while the husband goes to great lengths not to share or even admit that he has feelings. Of course, in same-sex relationships there is no gender distinction, but the roles exist just the same. One wants to talk until the wee hours of the night, and the other wants only to sleep and pretend that all is well.

Prognosis: If you are in denial about trouble in your relationship, if you're not interested in listening to your partner's concerns, keep in mind that there are always others who will be willing to listen. Don't say you didn't see it coming. Sure you did. You just didn't want to talk about it.

3.   **You Seem Nice, but Who Are You?**

In this relationship there are few shared interests, activities, or friends. There is no passion, either positive or negative. The couple merely coexists without real conflict, affection, or sexual satisfaction.

Prognosis: You may stay together but only due to inertia. Relationships and emotions at rest tend to stay at rest.

4.   **I Hate You...*I Love You...I Hate You*...I Love You!**

Fights worthy of a Hollywood epic are followed by makeup sex that shakes the rafters. Eventually, however, the intensity becomes almost unbearable on both ends of the spectrum.

Prognosis: Without long time-outs, one or both will collapse. Better than a relationship without any emotion but very shaky, and potentially dangerous when the makeup sex settles down to a subtle quiver. Watch out for Othello's green-eyed monster. Jealously will bite hard and gobble up both parties.

5.   One + One = 3

This is a relationship accented by warmth, consideration, and a sincere desire to help the other advance as an individual. This is a trusting relationship where each party can pursue independent goals and, at times, separate friendships. Requires a deep level of trust and a strong sense of self-worth.

Prognosis: Absolute nirvana, *if* both parties are secure, honest, open, willing to compromise, and highly sensitive to one another's needs. A rare relationship but worth the effort it takes to build and maintain.

It is interesting to note that women are most psychologically and physically sensitive to the various types of relationships. Women in the first three relationships suffer the most emotional and physical health problems. Significantly fewer troubles occur for women in volatile relationships, and little physical or psychological distress is in store for women in mutually supportive, clearly defined role relationships.

Men have a difficult time with the first two but suffer only negligible impact from the other types of relationships.

Of course it doesn't take a seven-figure government-sponsored study to show us that, overall, marriages and relationships accented by contempt, belligerence, denial, and withdrawal are doomed while those characterized by respect, trust, support, and value tend to flourish.

Friendships thrive in a field of support, understanding, and honesty. Relationships suffocate when negativity and cynicism override belief in the power of change and hope for the future. Yes, given enough time, kinks will appear in every suit of armor; some are little more than deep scratches while others are significant dents. Support can collapse under the weight of stress and tension, misunderstanding causes pain and confusion, and trust goes poof in the face of betrayal, deceit, and omission. Life. No excuse, just reality.

So what are among the key factors needed to grow and sustain a meaningful relationship? Here's my list:

- A core level of respect, love, and integrity

- Laughter

- You must like each other, *really* like each other

- Laughter

- A soulful belief that trust, once broken, can heal with time

- Laughter

- Forgiveness without malice, don't pick at scabs

- Laughter

- An active recognition that lingering guilt is self-serving and toxic for all parties

- Laughter
- Shared capacity and desire for lifelong learning and personal growth

Finally, did I mention laughter? A sense of humor helps immensely.

The baby…
crawls for the cat's tail
reaches for Mommy's arms
throws the oatmeal on the floor

The young child…
runs home after school
climbs a tree
jumps just for fun

The teenager…
dribbles the basketball
swings the racquet
slides into second base

The young adult…
hikes in the mountains
water skis on the lake
runs for a cause

The middle-aged adult…
sweats to the oldies
grunts for buns of steel
jogs the pounds away

The old man…
stretches to pick up the grandkids
lifts to push out the chair
walks to the kitchen for another bowl of oatmeal

EXERCISE FOR THE AGES

☼

EXACTLY WHEN DID EXERCISE BECOME A CHORE INSTEAD OF a delight? Okay, yes, yes, yes, for some of you, exercise is still a delight. But guess what? You are in the minority! Most adults, if held to the truth, would say it's a chore, a daily To Do that moves gradually from the top of the priority list to the bottom. In fact, it gives way to just about anything and is particularly vulnerable to "YeahBut" disease:

- Yeah, but I have to go shopping.

- Yeah, but it's raining.

- Yeah, but I'm really tired.

- Yeah, but I'm too busy.

- Yeah, but it's too late in the day.

- Yeah, but I just ate.

- Yeah, but I'm really hungry.

- Yeah, but my puppy ate my running shoes.

YeahBut disease is an equal opportunity affliction—rich, poor, boss, worker bee, educated, ignorant, black, white, whatever. It doesn't matter. It is also highly contagious.

Okay, so when does this YeahBut disease strike?

Certainly not when a child is a toddler. Just try keeping up with a little one when she's turned loose. For the young explorer, there are bugs to catch, cats to chase, pots and pans to bang, big kids to follow, food to throw, and furniture to climb. And all before lunch! She has no idea or concern that exercise is good for her. She moves to explore and to have fun.

Certainly not when a child is in elementary school. Try keeping a third grader in his seat learning how to add and subtract on a sunny day. There are frogs to catch, stones to throw, playground swings to conquer, shoes to scuff, puddles to jump, and cans to kick. And all before dinner! He doesn't know that exercise is good for him, and if you told him, he'd give you a blank look and go back to chasing the dog. He moves to thrive, to have fun.

Certainly not when kids hit middle school. There are soccer games to play, laps to swim, and ice rinks to skate. There are dance routines to rehearse, softballs to hit, basketballs to shoot, ropes to jump, skateboards to ride, malls to walk. And all before sitting down to do homework!

But wait, is this true of all kids at this age? No? Maybe we're onto something. The sad news is that by the time a child is in middle school, about twelve years old, the YeahBut disease is sweeping through the peer group at an incredible rate.

Adolescents exercise less than young children. Many preteens and teens consider it a chore or a punishment and don't connect physical activity with a personal interest. Gym class sucks.

Because of reduced exercise and horrible nutrition, childhood obesity has more than doubled in children and quadrupled in adolescents in the past thirty years. That's pretty amazing—frightening when you think about it. Where will today's obese kids be in another twenty years? All the gizmos and fad diets in the world won't be able to handle that much fat. That may sound cruel, but it's just scary when you think about the connection between diet, exercise, stress, and heart disease.

Certainly, inactive and obese kids have always been around (they have "glandular problems," baby fat, my dad is fat, and any number of explanations), but not in the numbers we see now.

Today's combination of pies, cakes, burgers, dogs, fries, pop, potato chips, the Internet, PlayStations, and TV add up to new levels of trouble. These last two, perhaps, being the biggest culprits. Oh yes, and the parents who hand off diet and activity responsibility to the schools, they are primary enablers.

WALKING THE THIN LINE BETWEEN CONFIDENCE AND HUBRIS

Long hours, impossible schedules, a family of strangers
Missed commitments, rescheduled appointments, a nagging headache
A longing for simplicity and fear that it will appear

Don't worry, I'll be fine…

Poor grades, vacant eyes, bare walls
Whisper-friends, wrinkled jeans, meals left on the table
Memory trips to smile with a little boy in a fireman's hat

Don't worry, he'll be fine…

Dishonest pleas, living by rote; courtesy replacing passion
Smiles for the guests, silence with the dishes, wonder replacing trust
A bed for two and sleep for neither

Don't worry, we'll be fine…

Taxes, nicks while shaving, kids who bring you smiles, less-than-stellar report cards, and sick hamsters. Traffic jams, rude clerks, the taste of hot dogs at the ball game, stomach acid, and the taste of Tums. Sore feet, eighty-year-old mothers who worry that you don't get enough sleep, socks that don't match, and other kinds of dogs with fleas. Life.

Strip away titles, clothes, cars, degrees, the stock market, stenciled parking spots, and first-class cabins. What do you have? A bunch of people talking about taxes, nicks while shaving, kids who bring you smiles, less-than-stellar report cards, and sick hamsters. Traffic jams, rude clerks, the taste of hot dogs at the ball game, stomach acid, and the taste of Tums. Sore feet, eighty-year-old mothers who worry that you don't get enough sleep, socks that don't match, and other kinds of dogs with fleas. Life.

Hubris is an excellent word. If you look it up in the dictionary, you'll see something like, excessive pride or arrogance. Look deeper and perhaps learn of its use in classic Greek tragedies where ruthless ambition and disregard of the limits that govern human actions lead to the hero's downfall. People with hubris make up their rules and spin convention to fit their personal needs.

I see it all the time, mostly from businesspeople, academics, and politicians jockeying for the top rung. Or from those who have made it to the top and wait impatiently for the coronation to begin. They look out over their conquered lands, mystified that the unwashed masses are not bowing in adulation or cowering in the presence of their brilliance.

There are, of course, excellent men and women who achieve both happiness and material success while maintaining perspective and respect for others. They're just hard to spot because they keep a low profile and share the limelight. They are too busy enjoying the intangible moments to grab the bullhorn and make public announcements.

Here are ten ways you can spot a hubristic person:

1. Behaves rudely or is condescendingly polite to subordinates and people who work in the service industries.

2. Carries the title of CEO home every night.

3. Takes credit for victories and chops off heads when things go wrong (at home as well as at work).

4. Believes social activities center around their needs.

5. Justifies virtually all actions in the name of the business or a particular cause.

6. Believes God is on their side.

7. Feels persecuted by those who just don't understand.

8. Doesn't get it when they see the billboard that reads, "What good is it if you are a success at business and a failure at home?"

9. Looks sad or angry when you see them, and they don't know it.

10. Ultimately separate and isolate themselves from those who care most about them.

The tragedy, of course, is that hubris often springs from a well of exceptional talent and vast potential. Arrogance generally comes on the heels of success and must be nurtured to bring it to full-blown hubris. If you want to be an enabler, here are ten things you can do to move someone along the path to heightened hubris:

1.   Regularly tell them how great they are and laugh at their sexist, racist, or stupid jokes.

2.   Make sure they get credit for all your successes.

3.   If they make a mistake, comfort them and take most of the blame. Remind them, again, how truly great they are.

4.   Tolerate their temperamental and rude behavior.

5.   Accommodate their selfish whims.

6.   Hide the facts and fix the problem.

7.   Compromise your personal and professional needs in favor of theirs.

8.   Convince yourself that the end justifies the means.

9.   Kid yourself that their behavior is only temporary.

10. Replace blinders every six months.

A hubris enabler is not very different from the neighbor of a mass murderer. The one who tells the police, "Well, I saw him putting guns and a bunch of ammunition in his trunk. Something that looked like a body but, hey, I figured it weren't none of my business. I sure ain't surprised, though."

Rather than be an enabler, here are ten things you can do to help someone conquer the habit of hubris:

1. Give them the opportunity to fail. Don't bail them out every time.

2. Never tolerate rudeness, cruelty, harassment, or misogyny.

3. Give straight answers.

4. Question decisions and behavior.

5. Take credit for your accomplishments.

6. Never compromise on personal integrity.

7. Tell the Emperor he is not wearing any clothes!

8. Speak up for those who cannot.

9. Take notes—you may need them.

10. When you sense that chronic hubris is heading into the terminal stage, run, don't walk, to the nearest exit. He's going down and he will try to take you with him.

Remember, just this side of arrogance and hubris is a wonderful business leader, life partner, parent, community spokesperson, mentor, and coach for all of us. If open to rescue, this person is worth saving. At the same time, don't kid yourself. You can point out the signs and warn him that the bridge is out, but only he can steer himself to safety. And if he does fall, who do you think he's going to blame on the way down? Bingo!

We are all, at times, a bit brusque with a salesperson or too quick to dismiss the opinion of a child or someone lacking formal education. It's unfortunate, but it happens. If we don't make a habit of it, it's no big deal. We should be more sensitive, of course, but at least we know it. A person with hubris, though, doesn't have a clue. With a sweep of his scathing, sarcastic scythe, he clears a swath big enough for his expanding ego, cutting down everyone in his path. You've been there when the guy screams at the ticket agent because an unexpected snowstorm has grounded his flight to Omaha. You've cringed when the mother, perhaps that same ticket agent, loudly berates her teenager in a room full of strangers. You've stood watching when the class mean girl—perhaps that same teenager embarrassed by her mother—laughs at the classmate who can't afford to buy designer clothes. Where do you suppose all these people learned to be mean, sarcastic, and condescending?

You're standing in front of a hotel in New York City waiting for a cab. One pulls up, the back door opens, and a man climbs out, yelling at the driver. He flings some bills through the driver's window and stalks away, muttering, "Stupid raghead." Somehow you know this guy will, with a snap of his fingers, spread his disease to the next waitress whose misfortune it is to serve him.

I am concerned, and I also feel pity. Such arrogance robs the offender of a vast spectrum of life resources. The cab driver whose name he couldn't pronounce, who he thinks should go back where he came from, along with all the other ignorant foreign laborers who infest his city, has a life the self-important, hubris-ridden passenger cannot imagine.

Take a ride with this cabbie. Ask him how he pronounces his name. Ask him about his homeland. You may learn that he is a highly educated chemist whose developing country has no money to hire him. You may discover that he is a hard-working, dedicated man who's here trying to make enough money to support his wife and kids back home. By showing interest, you'll learn something about a fellow citizen of your planet, something that will probably surprise you. You may also help him forget the insult from the guy who thinks all New York City cab drivers are illegal immigrants draining our resources.

Next time you get to the airport, flash a sympathetic smile and offer a kind word to that ticket agent; her day has been even longer than yours. Patience and a show of kindness may be good for her blood pressure as well as your own. Of course, courtesy is its own reward, but if you're truly civil, she might find you that last aisle seat on your connecting flight through Dallas.

Are you ready for another list of ten? Okay, here are ten things you can do to avoid hubris:

1. Ask a six-year-old to describe how you look.

2. Volunteer at a soup kitchen.

3. Change a lot of diapers.

4. Have a real conversation with someone from a developing nation.

5. Visit a retirement center or nursing home.

6. Talk to a cancer survivor.

7. Spend an hour with someone who knew you when.

8. Stay connected to your children.

9. Visit the Grand Canyon.

10. Go to another six-year-old and get a second opinion.

OVERCOMING THE PARALYSIS OF THE PROBABLE WITH THE POWER OF THE POSSIBLE

ERIK WEIHENMAYER. IN MAY 2001, I WAS AT THE MOUNT Everest base camp at the same time as Erik Weihenmayer. Erik reached the summit of the world's highest mountain on May 25. Erik is blind. Think about that for a second. Blind. Mount Everest. Summited.

When asked about this feat, he said, "I was confident I could do as well as anyone who goes to that mountain. And I knew I could turn back gracefully if necessary."

You don't have to have trekked to Mount Everest or climbed at high altitude to marvel at his accomplishment. Well, I've trekked to the Mount Everest base camp, and all I can say is: *Blind! Mount Everest! Summited! It's not possible!*

Jeff Rand. In July 2006, I celebrated my seventh year as a cancer survivor (thriver) by traveling to Africa and trekking to the true summit of Mount Kilimanjaro, Uhuru.

While all routes to the summit are difficult, it's 19,340 feet with approximately 50 percent of the oxygen measured at sea level, so the Machame route is particularly challenging. It is called the Whiskey Route. One of the others, the Marangu route is unfairly called the Coca-Cola Route. At any rate, trekking Kilimanjaro was even more challenging than my trek to the Everest base camp and the 18,192-foot summit of Mount Kala Patar.

Fact: Less than half of those who attempt the summit of Kilimanjaro succeed, and, each year, more people die on Kilimanjaro than die on Everest. Those African adventurers thought it would be easy. They were wrong. *Dead* wrong.

Jeff Rand was one of my Kili trekking partners in 2006. Jeff has trekked to the highest point in the forty-eight contiguous states and has logged mountain adventures throughout the world. The entire time in Tanzania, Jeff was positive, outgoing, supportive, and inspirational.

Inspirational? Oh, yes, did I forget to mention that Jeff only has one arm? Born that way. One arm. Think about that for a second. One arm. Stood on the highest point in forty-eight states. Summited Kilimanjaro, the highest freestanding mountain in the world, via the Whiskey Route. It's not possible!

Of course, the feats, like Erik and Jeff and millions of others accomplish in their lives, are not impossible. It's just that they are highly improbable. Ah, there it is again—possible versus probable. One is a factor of physics, and the other the sum of passion, support, and an opportunity.

How many times do you think that Eric and Jeff and friends were told: be practical, be reasonable, be content, be realistic. And worse: you'll never make it, never finish, never even come close.

Beware of people who use your failure to gauge the level of their success.

I continue my efforts to keep my knees healthy for another twenty years with hopes of reaching many more literal and figurative summits. People often tell me that, statistically, with my medical history, the probability is low that I will be able to continue high-altitude trekking into my seventies.

Oh, please, I'm not a blind mountaineer attempting to summit Mount Everest, and I'm not a mountain climber with only one arm. I'm just an extremely motivated guy with enormous professional and personal support. After all, I have Eric, Jeff, and hundreds of cancer thrivers loudly cheering for me, painting beautiful visions of success, and quietly whispering words of encouragement. I expect to do just fine, and I expect that you will do the same with your goals and aspirations as long as you overcome the paralysis of the probable with the power of the possible.

FEAR IS NOTHING MORE THAN SCARY STORIES WE TELL OURSELVES ABOUT THE FUTURE

IF YOU DON'T LIKE THE STORY LINE, REWRITE THE SCRIPT.

Not to get overly metaphysical, but all we ever have is this moment. The rest is either reflection about the past that increasingly distorts with time or conjecture about the future—in other words, pure fabrication, fiction, a story.

All too often we get entangled in self-told narratives filled with doom, gloom, and failure. We write the script, adjust the lighting, cue the sound effects, and scream, "Action!" We then sit back as the sole member of the audience and have the bejeebers scared out of us.

It's fiction! If you don't like the story line, rewrite the script.

Next time you start feeling anxious, make sure you guide your thoughts in a positive direction. Yes, it's still fiction, but it's an active, attractive fantasy that sparks a self-fulfilling prophecy leading to confidence and a sense of well-being.

One more time: It's fiction! If you don't like the story line, rewrite the script.

Or, of course, if you're a masochist, go ahead and keep scaring the bejeebers out of yourself (and those who live and work with you). It's your choice.

Five Ways to Get Productive Reactions from Stressful Situations

1. Gather the facts. When faced with a stressful situation, or you need to make a tough decision, step back for a minute. Then, gather all the information you need to analyze the problem or make an objective decision. Don't act impulsively—reserve judgment and action until you have all of the pertinent information. If you don't take a minute to gather the facts, your perceptions may be distorted causing confusion and wasted energy.

2. Assess responsibility and assume accountability. Recognize and acknowledge your role in creating potentially stressful situations. Constantly blaming others will alienate you from family, friends, and coworkers. With the right tools, you have a great deal of control over how you react to a stressful situation. However, refusing to accept accountability suggests that you do not have control over your life, and this lack of control makes you vulnerable to distress.

3. Make a plan and do something. You can waste time with fruitless dreaming or energy-draining complaining, or you can design a plan and take

action. Whether you are solving a complicated work problem or just deciding what to do this weekend, gather your facts and then make a plan of action. Tackle a large problem one step at a time. Of course, planning alone is not enough—after you decide what to do, you must follow through, or all your talk is just hot air.

4. Achieve and maintain physical fitness. A daily blend of exercise and proper nutrition is as close to a panacea as we can come. Improved self-esteem, a healthy respiratory and circulatory system, enhanced career opportunities, weight control, and longevity are just a sampling of the by-products of a regular regime of exercise and proper nutrition.

5. Maintain perspective. It is important to give each event an appropriate amount of weight and importance. What seems like an earth-shattering crisis today may be just a small hitch in your plans when reviewed tomorrow. As you deal with stressors, try to look at the whole picture. In the scope of things, what significance should you assign to the event or circumstances? Is it truly devastating? Is there zero hope for the future? There are always conditions for which we can be grateful and new opportunities that we can discover.

THE CANCER JOURNEY— TEN EMOTIONS

ALMOST SIXTEEN YEARS HAVE PASSED SINCE MY CANCER surgery and there isn't a day that goes by without acknowledging this journey at some level. In the beginning, this uninvited—and mind-numbing—voyage was distorted by a cracked prism of muted and blurred colors. When I squinted very hard, the view would suddenly burst forth with distinct edges and a hopeful clarity only to slip back into a murky and surreal world of distortion and confusion. The following sampling of emotions outlines where this road has taken me—or, better said, where I have chosen to go.

Shock

Cancer. The word is so horrific that it has become a metaphor for anything that is ugly, insidious, all consuming, and deadly. But, hey, it's only a metaphor, not the real thing. You know, an exaggeration for effect. Not the actual thing, not the pathology, the disease, the Big *C* that got Uncle Tim.

And then someone says the word in the same sentence as you.

I'm sorry, what did you say? Cancer? Me? I have cancer?

Both the question and the head-nod response seem to echo as if whispered loudly in a hollow tube placed too close to my ear. The volume is fine, but surely I misunderstood. I'm sorry, what did you say? I begin to float. Time is just a word that rhymes with dime and the echoes grow loud.

Denial and Detachment

There must be a mistake.

No, he said. No mistake. Your test was positive; you have cancer. I'm thinking—no.

Okay. Yes. But it isn't that bad, right? I mean, not like what killed Uncle Tim. Not what we think about when we hear the word *cancer*. At least, not in this case, my case. Right?

You're sure? Well, what does it mean? What do we do now? What do I do now? Your office, as soon as possible? Sure, okay. (pause) What does this mean, again?

Are you sure?

Why do they call the test result positive?

Sadness and a Profound Sense of Impending Loss

I take things for granted. There is a future. I will grow old with my best friend; I will watch my kids grow up. I will play with my grandchildren. I will retire. I will, I will, I will...

Then, again, maybe there is no future. I won't grow old with my best friend; I won't watch my children grow up. I won't play with my grandchildren. I won't retire. I won't, I won't, I won't...

I miss them already. The pain comes in waves and hits me in the stomach. Hard. I can't breathe.

Fear

I'll shave my head before I watch it fall out. On second thought, no. I'll hold on to every hair I can.

Oh, God. I'm frightened. I don't want to die. Not now. Not ever. But particularly, not now.

Will I have to have chemo? Will it make me sick? Will I retch in the corner wanting to die?

Oh, God. I'm frightened. I don't want to die. Not now. Not ever. But particularly, not now.

Spirituality

I don't remember it that blue. The sky. I don't remember it that blue. A forever blue…

Okay God, time to talk. What can I do? What do you want me to do? And why? Is this random? Is there a purpose and, if so, what?

The flower is so very delicate. The colors spread out gorgeous with perfect symmetry. The artist took such great care. I don't remember ever seeing that silky texture before. So smooth like a fine powder.

What if you don't exist? What if all of this is just a frenetic spiral of activity without purpose, without thought, without consequence? What then? Who will listen? Who will care?

The rolling thunder used to sound so peaceful, now it just sounds lonely and lost like a child wondering without hope. The voice that was once forceful, demanding, confident, and in control is now muffled and questioning, growing faint in the distance.

I don't remember it that blue. The sky. I don't remember it that blue. A deep, forever blue…

Okay, God, time to talk. You name the terms.

Anger

What will be, will be. I will be like the Brits—lip stiff and head held high. I will accept this with quiet dignity and count my blessings.

Wrong. I'm angry. I'm so mad I can't see straight. At this point, quiet resolution seems obscene and, in many ways, too easy, too convenient. Yes, I am frightened, frustrated, and confused. But— hear it again—I am angry. I am so mad I can't see straight. So screw the Brits. I'm not ready, not yet.

Cancer, you are a sneak and a thief, and you just broke into my house. My house! Well, get ready for a fight. The poet was right; I will not go gently into that good night. Screw the Brits and screw cancer!

Bring it on.

Analytical Focus

Statistics and probabilities, anecdotes and home cures, speculation and facts. Tons of advice and deafening silence.

I want to know everything I can about my cancer, this thing that is living in me, this rude and unwelcome guest. I want to know its size, how fast it is growing, how it got here, and—more than anything else—how to get rid of it.

Did you know that ___ people get this cancer, every year? Last year ___ people died with this disease. ___ were my age, and the risk factors are x, y, and z. The treatment options are ___, ___ and ___.

In addition to traditional therapies, ___ is being done in Asia.

Some guy on the Internet suggested ___, and Bill, my neighbor, said his uncle said his doctor told him to try ___.

The world goes on hold. I am becoming my cancer. I can feel it devouring me. I hate it and, yet, I am drawn to it like an abusive lover. I want nothing to do with it, but I can't get it out of my mind. It invades the most intimate and vulnerable chambers of my soul and won't let go.

What's the old saying, stay close to your friends and even closer to your enemies? I will know this enemy, I will go eyeball to eyeball with the son of a bitch and I will not blink.

Reentry (Excitement, Fear, Confusion, Resolve)

Patiently waiting. After the surgery, after the meds, after the pain, after the cards and well-wishers, life sits…patiently waiting.

Immediately after denial and intellectualization comes the creeping, then leaping thought that I might die. Every twitch, every cough, every bump, every everything confirms this. No, there's no maybe about it; I am going to die soon.

 Your margins are clean, says the doc. Your chances of living a long and healthy life are looking good. Pearl Harbor, the Kennedy Assassination, 9/11. After a defining event life is never the same, not really. You have cancer. Life is not the same. So what does, "I'm going to live" mean now? I don't know; I'm not sure. Different, I do know that. Better? I hope so. More finely tuned? I know so.

Obligation and Responsibility

Why was it caught in time, this cancer, this Monster? Why am I here? This is an age-old question with a new twist. I could have died; perhaps, statistically, I should have died. But here I am. I can't believe (choose not to believe) that the universe is random. Things do happen for a reason. The path is usually right in front of us, but we keep mucking up the view, making it harder than it needs to be.

One thing is sure. I feel an obligation, a welcome duty to live life just a bit fuller—okay, a whole lot fuller. I take care of myself even better than before. I take chances, not foolish physical chances, but chances outside my comfort zone. You know, the *wouldas, couldas,* and *shouldas* of life. I've left Walter Mitty to dream in the easy chair while I do things.

I also feel a responsibility to help others. Not just those with the Big *C* but those with the metaphoric *C* as well—words of encouragement, a telephone call, a dollar where a dollar matters. Mostly, however, I feel the responsibility to demonstrate my life as a collection of moments…not years.

Perspective

Broken dishwasher, flat tire, disagreeable strangers, bad cold, rainy weather, Ohio State beats Michigan, again. Bummer, but it ain't cancer!

FRIENDSHIP

When you know it's right to say, You're wrong
When you're able to hear, You're wrong, when you think you're right
Gently hold and release without question

A call at three a.m. with no need to explain
Silent tears without fear of interruption
Knowing what not to say

No favors, only gestures of caring and affection
Where respect drowns out judgment
Where trust washes over suspicion

I have friends of all shapes and sizes. I have sports friends, movie friends, family friends, cancer friends, old friends, travel/mountain-climbing friends, Facebook friends, and pet friends (as in our dog, Chaucer, and our cat, Willie). Some friends fit into several categories, others just one.

For the most part, my friends are very different people, and not necessarily close friends with each other; acquaintances, yes, but not friends. I'm not sure if that makes me eclectic, diverse, schizophrenic, tolerant, fragmented, indecisive, or just plain lucky. I'll go with just plain lucky.

Tech Friend

When I simply want to give in to the pestering and impish pleadings of the little boy inside (who disguises himself as this middle-aged guy with white hair), I call my tech friend Jeff. We head over to Best Buy or surf Amazon looking for gadgets. No different from when, as ten-year-old kids, Jack Runfola and I used to wander through the sixth floor of Bigelow's Department Store on Third Street in Jamestown. Aisles and aisles filled with paint-by-number kits, Lincoln Logs, Lionel model trains, Silly Putty, erector sets, miniature cars, and all kinds of Davy Crockett stuff. We never had more than just enough pop-bottle money for a couple of jawbreakers at the candy counter on the second floor, but it was still fun to look.

Problem is that today I do have money. Well, maybe not, but I have credit cards—lots of them. And that's just as good, right?

Coonskin caps and chemistry sets have given way to iPhones, digital cameras, and big-screen televisions. By myself, I am a coward; I give way to reason. I hesitate with thoughts of mundane things, like property taxes and retirement living. But with a simple lift of both eyebrows from my buddy and his quick triple nod of encouragement, the credit card jumps out of my wallet. Don't worry, if that one gets rejected, I have plenty more.

Then I hear the sound of the register singing back a code that says, sure, we'll take his lifelong interest payments at 18.5 APR. What a rush!

Ah, Silly Putty was never this much fun. Thanks, Jeff! Just don't tell Hillary, okay?

Old Friends

There are old friends, and there are friends who are old. In my case, they are quickly running together. That's good. I like it that way. I get the benefit of their life wisdom as well as the value of our scrapbook memories.

We knew each other when

- We sneaked cigarettes behind Dave Marsh's garage.

- We played Spin the Bottle with Patty, Joanne, Beth, and Nancy.

- We made crank phone calls about Prince Albert and running refrigerators.

- Sister Mary Louise slapped Tom McGowan, and we didn't know why, and neither did he.

- Joe came up with one more excuse why he couldn't go swimming during gym class.

- My sister disappeared, died, and I felt my grasp on the world slip.

- I enlisted during the Vietnam War because I was frightened, felt alone, and didn't know which way to turn.

- I got out of the military and met Hillary and my soul at the same time.

- My incredible children appeared.

- The order of life changed after the death of my parents.

- Dr. Marcus said, "Michael, you have cancer."

- Responsibility caught up with me—or was it the other way around?

These are the friends who laugh when someone pays you too much respect. They bring up long-forgotten nicknames and begin sentences with whatever happened to _____? and gosh, do you remember when _____? For the moment, you are once again seven, twelve, twenty-three, or thirty-two.

In a memory flash, the place where you're standing becomes Diamond 1 at Vet's Park. It's the bottom of the ninth, two outs, and you're the only chance we have to beat Kalamazoo Central. Or you're standing on the gymnasium dance floor wishing you had the nerve to ask Sandy for the next slow dance. Or maybe it's biology class, and Mr. Scruggs leans too close to the Bunsen burner and sets his tie on fire—again. Or you and your buddy are in Principal Maybe's office, and you both say at the same time, "It wasn't me, sir, honest, you can ask anyone!"

With each scene, you hear the voices, recapture the feelings, and search for similar moments. Together, you freeze-frame time until the motion of the day breaks in to remind you of the things you need-should-ought to do.

Time to return to this life—but thanks for the moments, old friend.

Old and New

I once did a book reading and signing at Borders, the bookstore in Ann Arbor, Michigan. At the time, I had lived in the area for forty years or more, so, for this hometown kid, there was a larger than usual crowd for an author reading.

As I looked into the audience, I saw among the crowd four decades of friendships and memories. What must they have been thinking? Each smile said something different as their eyes flickered with eight-millimeter movies taken long ago. Some must have shaken their heads and whispered to themselves, *Who'd a thunk it, Sam, a published author?*

Others quietly remembered my family. Still others were simply curious patrons who wandered upstairs to see who was speaking. My guess is that they all looked around the room and wondered, *Who are all these people?*

That was the most surprising part. Here was a room filled with many of the most important people in my life, and they did not know each other. There were Kathy and her daughter, Julie, neighbors when our children were small. My business partner, Tom, who is more brother than associate. Bob was there, a friend, going all the way back to Tappan Junior High, an easy 3:00 a.m. qualifier. Bob's mother, Peg, attended as well. She was so kind to me as a kid barging in her side door after school.

A special attendee was Tim Harbour and his family. Tim remains an inspiration captured in this book. My wife's family, mine as well for the past thirty years; my children; and the current dinner-movie-barbecue gang.

How could they not have met over all these years? I believe it's because friends have a way of drawing out and dancing with different parts of our personalities. Some make us laugh, so we look for them when we're feeling a bit blue. Some make us think, so we call them when we're in the mood for some intellectual diversion, like a foreign film at the Michigan Theater. Most are as comfortable as old slippers and a ratty robe; we welcome them anytime. Others require higher maintenance, best seen when the energy tank is full. Some are great in groups, and others are strictly one-on-one.

The book I was reading at Borders was *Voices from the Edge*. It's a book featuring cancer patients who faced death with dignity, humor, and a profound appreciation for the pure offerings of life. The poem I recited at the end of the reading spoke of their courage and spirit. As I finished, I looked out to see individual faces. I felt pulled in all directions. The energy of that moment stays with me to this day. The memory of that moment will remain with me for a lifetime.

Best Friends

There are those special people we call best friend. When I was a kid, the title circulated from Jack Runfola to Patty Powers, to George Collins, to John Herbein, to Jeff Griffith, to John Myers, then around again. Patty dropped out of the best category when it became too apparent that she was not a boy. Remember, this was the 1950s. Boys didn't play with girls.

These were the neighborhood guys who shared with me such coming-of-age moments as snapping girls' bra straps. Suzie still wore T-shirts in the sixth grade, but Mary and Annette were fair game. Other early adolescent energy went into puppy love for Janie, terrorizing the Sisters of Mercy, sneaking a little wine from the sacramental cruets, and gagging on our first cigarettes, stolen from the little green store on the corner of Fairview and Harding.

For me, the 1950s in Jamestown, New York, was all about secret pacts, wonder, pickup baseball games, harmless mischief, and best pals forever. And then some of us moved away, and we all grew up—well, at least some of us did.

When I moved to Ann Arbor at age fifteen, my Tappan Junior High best friends became John, Pete, and Erik. Weekends brought more cigarettes, more booze ("Hey, Mister, will you buy us a six-pack? You can have one."). Continuing adolescence meant more immature lusting, more lying, and a lot more self-discovery. It was a time for young adult male intimacy in the form of insults and nicknames. Sarcasm and wisecracks were the subtle codes that let us guys safely express emotion and reveal our personal beliefs, attitudes, and aspirations. In other words, we could become more intimate without acknowledging that this was what we were doing. Remember, the early to mid-1960s were highly homophobic times. Better be careful. Got to keep the insults coming fast and furious. And for God's sake, don't hug me!

High school was much the same, but girlfriends broke up most of the guy time we had before. Singles became couples: Linda and Pete, Sue and John, Cheryl and Erik, and Margo and me. An interesting side note: After college, all of the other couples married. Margo and I went our separate ways, but remain close friends after all these years.

During the Vietnam era, close friends changed from base to base. We all needed someone to share our complaints, help us find girls in the local towns, and commiserate when the wise young ladies told us to get lost. We needed each other to tell us when we were wrong, laugh at our stupid jokes, help us back to the barracks after too many beers at the Airmans Club, and lend us twenty bucks till payday. We also needed someone to get drunk and cry with when we heard that a buddy had been killed two weeks after stepping off a C-130 in Da Nang.

Not always a pretty picture, but, hey, we were twenty-one and in the military, and it was 1969. During that year, Apollo 11 landed on the moon. Charles Manson slaughtered Sharon Tate and six others. Dinner was served with nightly broadcasts of body bags unloading at Dover AFB. The New York Mets won the World Series, and half a million people hung out for a weekend on some guy's farm in Bethel, New York.

Then, as now, sharing time with friends and family gives life texture and context. Otherwise it's just a lot of sand running through the hourglass.

CHILDREN: YOURS, MINE, AND OURS, FOREVER

BUSY WITH LIFE. VERY TIRED. HUNGRY.
Many things to do

It's not my fault. It's not my fault.
It's not my fault. Besides…

Look straight ahead and become invisible;
Close your heart and become blind

Excuse me, sir, whispers the man who sees
into and through me

Guilt, embarrassment, insecurity, courtesy,
annoyance, or perhaps a shared echo

Eyes meet and I'm trapped. Souls meet
and I'm, what? Free?

He is a stranger, yet I know him well
He is not from this country, yet we are neighbors

He carries the scars but, curiously,
I share the pain

I turn to look into his eyes and I see a brother
I open my heart and see myself

There are children, he whispers, who need our help
could I please…

The words are soft and low; the urging is quietly
accented with both desperation and hope

Searching for my face, his scarred eyes see only blurs and shadows
while the cinema of memory replays vivid scenes of terror
The faded television star tells us that for
only one dollar a day…

Distended bellies in Biafra, homeless in
Kosovo, Sister Mary Ada's plea for pagan babies

What is it this time that holds me and makes it
so easy to give?

Kindness in the face of brutality,
hope in the face of despair,

Trust in a world of sinister shadows

A solitary craft in a violent sea of immeasurable
depth with horrific monsters

There are children, he whispers, who need our help
could I please…

Through a thinning gauze of righteous denial
I write the check, but he wants more

Money wins today's battle, but only
knowledge and outrage will win the war

I turn to leave and perhaps to quickly forget,
but his gentleness holds me

I have not seen my children for two years, he says.
I cannot return home
and they are not free to leave…

Home is spoken with resolute sadness and
free to leave with determination

His smallness in the large lobby is balanced
by the size of his will and commitment

The force of his quiet message drowns out
the noise of indifference

As I rush home to hug my kids,
I hear his soft roar as he frees the soul of
another familiar stranger

I wrote this opening poem in July of 2001, immediately after arriving home one night from a long business trip. I'll ask you to revisit that night, shortly, but first, a little perspective.

> *Raw (adj), uncooked; in natural condition; not processed; inexperienced; damp, sharp, or chilly.* (Webster's Dictionary and Thesaurus)

Yes, I think that describes children quite nicely. They are raw and, at least in the beginning, innocent and pure.

Confession time: I love kids. I love little kids, big kids, funny kids, sad kids, kids who like me, kids who don't (sometimes I like those the best). Black, white, yellow, red, purple, green, and spotted. I love kids with mohawks, brush cuts, ponytails, and carved numbers. And I don't care if the hair is black, white, yellow, red, purple, green, or spotted. Well, okay, if someday a grandchild came over to the house with a spotted green Mohawk, I probably would not like it. But I'd still hug, love, and accept him or her.

Sometimes children drive me crazy, break my heart, empty my wallet, test my patience, and make me look twice every time I pass a mirror and catch the color of my hair. But I would go nuts without them, all of them—yours, mine, and ours. Forever.

Autumn 1956

I pounce on life every day from the center of my universe: 119 Hall Avenue, Jamestown, New York. I eat it up! I have two older brothers—Paul, seventeen, and David, ten—and an older sister, Mary Jo (she hates that name, so we call her

Dodie). I have a dog, Taffy, who, like all dogs in 1956, runs free in the neighborhood. I have two parents who love me.

Catholic or not, they will have no more kids after me, and I am spoiled rotten. I love every minute of it! Norman Rockwell could have put us on the cover of the *Saturday Evening Post.* I'm the one with the freckles, reddish-blond hair, and a homemade slingshot hanging out of his back pocket. Well, sometimes it was a peashooter tucked behind my ear or, often, a magnifying glass for burning initials into a block of wood or other things done by eight-year-old boys that you don't want to know.

Of course, life is a lot like a magazine. It has a thin cover, and what's inside doesn't always live up to the colorful cover shot. Also, things are not as clear when you look through the wrong end of the telescope—but that's for another time. For now, I'm an eight-year-old kid armed with all my toys, and, for the most part, life is great.

Hey, television's getting better and better. Not only can you hear Patti Page sing the "Tennessee Waltz" or "How Much Is That Doggie in the Window?" you can now see her on the *Lucky Strike Hit Parade.* She's pretty. I can't quite figure out why, but it's not the same as my mom being pretty.

Elvis is on the *Ed Sullivan Show.* Mom likes him; Dad doesn't. Dodie sure does, but I don't think she wants Dad to know that. As for me, I want to be just like him when I grow up. Elvis or Mickey Mantle. Mickey just won the Triple Crown! He said that the summer of 1956 was his favorite. I get that. I had a blast! Most of the time, I was on cloud nine!

Also, on television, we get *Felix the Cat, Howdy Doody, The Lone Ranger,* and for the grown-ups, shows like *This Is Your Life* and *Queen for a Day*. On *Queen for a Day*, a guy named Jack Bailey makes some lady from the audience Queen. He gives her stuff like washing machines and vacuum cleaners. Of course, to be the Queen she has to convince everyone that she is poor and miserable.

If she cries a lot, the audience cries too and applauds like crazy when he holds the crown over her head. Then the applause meter arm goes way up, and she gets the refrigerator and the crown. The best show was when they crowned the lady who didn't have any legs. Her husband got killed in the war; she could see out of only one eye, and all seven of her kids were sick because she didn't have any money to buy medicine or food. She was great! They didn't have any refrigerators, so I think they gave her a trip to Florida or something like that. My Grandma Hayes loves this show. Won't miss a day.

When it comes to television, I like everything, even all those commercials for cigarettes. I especially like the one where Fred and Barney go behind the barn to hide from Wilma and Betty. They watch the girls mow the lawn while they smoke a couple of Winstons. Winstons were my dad's favorite brand. And Kent cigarettes were my mom's favorite; they were the ones with the Micronite filters.

Third grade at St. Pete's is okay. I get to play dodgeball in the gym (I'm almost always the last one standing). The nun who teaches me looks like a penguin, but she hits like Floyd Patterson. At least I think she's a she. The school has an old boiler that breaks down a lot, so we get a bunch of free days to stay home in the winter. I can read pretty well, but Sister Mary Gracias says that *Mad* magazine does not count and is not allowed in school. I have it anyway. I just hide it in my notebook.

On Fridays, we bring quarters to rescue pagan babies. My row never seems to win. The third row saved five babies already, and it's only November. Sister says we're not trying hard enough, and God knows it.

On Saturdays, we all have to go to confession so our souls will get scrubbed clean. Then we can do what we want the rest of the week. I confess to telling lies, punching the little kid down the street, stealing *Mad* magazines from Davis Drug Store, and buying candy with the money my mom gives me for those poor pagan babies.

O, my God, I am heartily sorry for having offended Thee. I detest all my sins because of your just punishment, but most of all because they offend you, my God, who are all good and deserving of all my love. I firmly resolve, with the help of Your Grace, to sin no more and to avoid the near occasion of sin.

Ten Hail Marys, ten Our Fathers, and a trip around the Stations of the Cross and I'm good for another week.

At home, I think things are pretty good. Dad comes home every night about the time *Howdy Doody* ends, and we eat at six o'clock sharp. I sneak Taffy my lima beans, so my plate is clean, and I can get some dessert. My older brother, Paul, talks about girls and a guy named Ginsberg. My dad says he's a beatnik and a bum. (No, not my brother, the Ginsberg guy.) My sister, Dodie, talks about boys and Johnny Mathis. My dad says that Johnny Mathis is a queer. I'm not sure what a queer is, but I know my dad doesn't like them so they must be bad. David doesn't talk much. I try to get them all to laugh so they won't see me sneak the lima beans to Taffy.

After dinner, we do the dishes, say the rosary, and pray for a lot of things like Aunt Margaret Madden's hip and the conversion of Russia. My knees hurt, so I sit back on my heels.

"Mike! Kneel up straight!" says my dad as he whacks me on the butt. He used to be a Lutheran.

After the last amen, we watch the end of Walter Cronkite. Night after night, right before he says, "And that's the way it is!" we see things happening all over the world and sometimes talk about them. We see tanks in some place called Hungary. What a funny name for a country! We see a humongous bomb exploding over an island where nobody lives (not anymore, I think to myself). And we see more pictures from last year when that colored lady wouldn't let a white guy have her seat on a bus. My dad says that's all over now, and anybody can do anything they want, even if colored. I ask him if that includes Mr. White, the nice, old colored guy with the gold tooth. He comes by every once in a while and asks if we have any junk we don't want.

There's also lots of newsreel film on Walter Cronkite showing that Russian guy, Kerchief (another funny name). Mom says he looks like Uncle Ray. And Uncle Walter is always talking about a soldier with a beard. He smokes cigars, like Uncle Paul. The soldier guy wants to kick the bad guys out of Cuba. Everyone hopes he does.

Some questions from an eight-year-old living in the year, 1956:

- Why do all the colored people live behind Fairmount Avenue or over by Love School? And why are their clothes too small for them, and why do their houses need painting?

- Why did they take away that nice man who lives on Fairview? Was it because he helped that little girl go to the bathroom?

- Why does my face get hot and red when Susie Whitmore talks to me?

- Why do we have to take Dad's beer bottles to the dump every year?

- Do the nuns wear anything under their penguin suits?

- Why do Mom and Dad yell at each other so loudly that I have to cover my ears to go to sleep?

- What's a queer?

- Why can't a pagan baby go to heaven?

- How come Monsignor Tobin told John Myers and me that we couldn't visit the nice man from the Jewish temple at the top of the hill? He was teaching us to write our names in Hebrew. When we told him we couldn't come back, he looked a little sad but smiled and told us to respect our priest. I don't know why we can't go there anymore, but Monsignor Tobin doesn't like that place, and my mom says he's a walking saint, so...

- What's wrong with *Mad* magazine, anyway?

September 1976

A blink. Twenty years. Hillary and I celebrate our fourth wedding anniversary, and I graduate with a master's degree in guidance and counseling from the University of Michigan Rackham School of Graduate Studies. I start working in a school system as a guidance counselor. The kids in my office are the messed up ones. I don't care if they take geometry or algebra II; I just want to them to survive high school.

I begin a doctoral program at Michigan that I later leave to help launch a health promotion company that I manage for twenty-five years.

I witness the birth of our first child; wake almost every day with the memory of my sister's horrible death on March 19, 1975. I drink much too much beer and wince a bit when I see any nun in traditional habit.

I repress anger for fear of rejection. I feel a mixture of respect and resentment for priests, smoke two packs a day, and continue with my strange fascination and affection for Jewish history and the Jewish religion. I have nurture/nature arguments with students and rest my case on the side of life.

Oh, and I also take delight in satire including a new television show called *Saturday Night Live*. I enjoy an occasional clandestine peek at *Mad* magazine.

July 2001

I uncurl my six-foot-two-inch, 210-pound body out of 23B (a middle seat in coach). I struggle with my carry-on baggage and do the all-too-familiar stutter-step waltz up the tube aisle of the Boeing 737. All I can do is think of home. The trip has been a long one; I am tired and a bit cranky. I'm looking forward to seeing my family, grabbing a bite to eat, and flopping down on the couch with a good book or a bad television show.

The last thing I want is to confront my conscience or feel tugs at the old heartstrings. I am in no mood for reality. But there he is. Short, black suit, shabby scuffed shoes, medium build, holding a notebook close to his chest with both hands.

I don't know his name, and—sorry—I probably couldn't pronounce it correctly if I saw it. But no matter, I see him, and he sees me. Or, perhaps more accurately, he senses me. I lower my head to run the gauntlet of travelers, well-wishers with balloons, airline personnel, and guys holding up signs that read Schmansky, Jones, and Dutch Travel.

"Excuse me, sir," he says. "There are children who need our help."

He knows I see him, our eyes meet, and, most compelling, I hear him.

"Excuse me, sir," he says again, stepping forward. "There are children who need you. Could you please help them?"

As I put down my bags and reach to find a dollar or two to block any deeper flow of emotion, he opens the notebook to show me his papers: who he is and who he represents. He assures me that his is a legitimate cause and that he has permission to solicit in the airport. Honestly, at that moment, I don't care. I simply want to give him a couple of bucks so I can feel righteous and go home.

He doesn't want my two dollars. He wants three hundred dollars. Excuse me. What? I stammer. He explains that three hundred dollars is what is required to save one child from Saddam Hussein's tyranny, to fly one child out of the country to be reunited with family.

I have not seen my daughter for over two and a half years, and there are many other parents who have not seen their children for longer than that. A political dissident, he was tortured, then tossed out of the country along with several others who protested Saddam's government. Hunch backed. Damaged eyes. He cannot define features, only blurry shapes.

I can feel my inner cynic, and his liberal-when-convenient partner, emerge for a moment. They shake their heads and turn away, one muttering something about the crime of using children as part of a scam, the other whimpering about the futility of it all.

But I quickly shove them back inside and hold them down while I dig out my checkbook. Their muffled voices nag at me. My daughter needs more clothes for her laundry heap; there's another must-have gadget with my name on it at Best Buy; I have my family and myself to consider.

What finally kills these contrary voices within is the picture. Not the photo of his child, but the whole picture: he's standing in an airport on a Friday night, putting his shoe leather, time, and humility behind his commitment. To me it feels somehow different from Sally Struthers's 2:00 a.m. cable television plea. I can't explain how; it's just different. Perhaps it's because I can feel his humanity, his sincerity. It's just a feeling, I've learned to trust that feeling.

As I fold the receipt, I do not sense righteousness or relief. Nor do I sense any awe at my magnanimous gesture and great personal sacrifice. He has more souls to stop; time is growing short. What I do sense is my gratitude for the lessons shared; for the home on Village Road with the front porch light turned on for me. And I feel grateful for my magical friend and wife, Hillary, our tail-wagging old dog, Boomer, an indifferent cat named Mozart, and the children that I will soon hold—very tightly.

Most of the bumps carried from childhood are smoothed away by experience, maturity, and humility. But the impact of childhood never leaves. We push back and deny the pain, forgive the ignorance, and, as parents, promise to do our best not to make the same mistakes our parents made.

By the way, if you are a parent, don't think for a moment that what you do doesn't affect your kids. I know. I heard your kids' stories when I was a summer camp director. I witnessed the day-to-day wear when I was a classroom teacher. And I counseled your crying and suicidal children as a high school guidance counselor.

As a parent, your attitude, language, relationships with others, and view of life stay with your kids, no matter how much they try to shake it. Will a difficult childhood ruin their lives? Probably not. Will they forget? At a conscious level, yes, some of it. Will they shape their view of life based on what they experienced in your home? Yes, without a doubt.

Have I made mistakes? Certainly. Will I make more? Yes, of course. Will my children ever question my love, dedication, and commitment to their lives? I pray the answer is always no. Will I ever throw a kid out of my house? Sure, if one of them shows up wearing a green spotted Mohawk! Just kidding.

January 2015

In all my experience with children, the biggest thrill continues to be fatherhood. Brent, Derek, and Logan are the fabric of my soul, and I love them dearly. With Hillary, we still talk, share, laugh, cry, get angry, and hug. We are truly present in one another's lives. The three will forever be my friends as well as my children, and the same goes for the grandchildren.

Note: In 1996, my mother, who smoked those Kent cigarettes, died with emphysema. You remember Kent cigarettes, the ones with the Micronite filters? Well, along with all the known horrors of tobacco, those Micronite filters contained asbestos. This has nothing to do with children; I just thought you might want to know. Oh, and my dad with his Winstons? He got lung cancer, lost both legs from peripheral vascular disease caused by too much booze and too many cigarettes, and died at age sixty-eight. Again, nothing to do with children; I just thought you might want to know.

Come to think of it, the tobacco cautionary tale has everything to do with children.

LANCE ARMSTRONG: CANCER, BETRAYAL, AND DECEIT. IT'S NOT ABOUT THE BIKE

NOTE: AS THIS REFLECTION UNFOLDS, IT WILL NOT BE FROM a cast-the-first-stone perspective. I am far from an archetype of virtue. I've made mistakes, I've wished for do-overs, and, I would guess, so have you. This reflection is not a judgment crusade. After all ultimately—who am I, who are we, to judge? I don't know about you, but final judgment, when all is said and done, is way above my pay grade.

Let's just see where this takes me. Seriously, there is such a confluence of emotion that I need to put fingers to the keyboard and let it flow.

Disappointment, anger, concern, empathy, outrage, sympathy, confusion, and back again to disappointment. And that's just nicking the surface.

For over ten years, a framed poster presented to me by the Lance Armstrong Foundation hung proudly and prominently in our home in Michigan, and in the boardroom of the Health and Wellness Institute in Rhode Island. After retiring from HWI in 2010, the poster once again was displayed in our home in Michigan. It is an announcement of a cancer survivor event in Austin where I proudly and gratefully shared the stage with Lance Armstrong and Lisa Bashore.

Since that Saturday afternoon in Austin on April 7, 2001, I've delivered scores of cancer survivorship talks throughout the nation including additional presentations at the request of Livestrong, formally known as the Lance Armstrong Foundation. I also participated in a Tour of Hope cycling event, a fifty-mile ride into Washington, D.C.—led by Armstrong—to raise cancer awareness and funds for survivor support. It was always my honor to contribute to this cause anytime, anywhere. Whenever Armstrong, the Foundation, and Livestrong asked, whenever any cancer organization asked, the answer was and always is, without hesitation, yes.

Say it ain't so…

Following Lance's chat with Oprah back in January 2013, I dressed down the screened image of Armstrong with venom-sprayed expletives. The lies, the arrogance, the vindictive trampling of good people whose only crime was telling the truth at the risk of clenched-jawed Armstrong wrath, sycophant lawyers serving papers, and mercurial public scorn.

Perhaps, most of all, the flood of emotion was because he pulled out an egotistical and hubris needle and popped a balloon of trust. He vaporized a poetic illusion. For years, he cultivated comparisons with another Armstrong. Jack Armstrong. The All-American Boy, born in Radioland, USA, on July 31, 1933, a star athlete at Hudson High School, international superstar, and universal role model.

But that was fiction, our Armstrong was real! He was the Olympian, cancer survivor, and Tour de France Champion, born in Plano, Texas, on September 18, 1971, a star athlete at Plano East Senior High School, international superstar, and universal role model.

Yes! Yes! Yes! We want and need our heroes. Take a bow, Lance Armstrong, take a bow!

But, wait a minute, what's that you say? This mythic, perfect story was one big lie. You say that you cheated during every one of your seven Tour de France victories; that you bullied, threatened, and intimidated those with the courage to speak the truth; that you just didn't believe that, in spite of all your admissions, you were cheating!

And, to add to your crinkled armor and tin foil crown, authorities say that you, our disgraced liar and cheat, hit two parked cars after a night of partying in Aspen but let your girlfriend, Anna Hansen, take the blame, to lie for you.

Ah, say it ain't so, Lance. Please, say it ain't so.

Oh, never mind, you don't need any more encouragement to lie. Just, please, go away.

If it seems too good to be true…

No matter how much it served our personal yearning for real-world, honest-to-goodness caped crusaders, the Lance Armstrong story was simply too good to be true. Deep down, we knew it. As with the creeping credibility collapse of *Three Cups of Tea* author, Greg Mortenson (too good to be true), the heroic level of the cancer survivor turned seven-time Tour de France conqueror defied reason. But favoring the comforting gauze of wished-for miracles and Wheaties fanfare, the facts, logic, and preponderance of evidence were screened, pushed aside, and hushed by the desire, hope, and, yes, naiveté, of millions. Duped, but willingly so.

Lance was not the only beneficiary of these self-serving actions. Hubris cannot live without an adoring audience anxious to elevate those who defy the outer limitations decreed by the gods. Shame on you, Lance Armstrong, and, to a lesser, cautionary degree, shame on us, as well. Together we created a parasitic symbiosis that only the bravest among us had the courage to acknowledge, separate, and expose the toxic relationship.

Yes, Virginia, real heroes do exist…

Actually, maybe now is a good time to stop bestowing the rank of hero on anyone who just does the right thing—you know, the stuff our moms told us to do when we were little. Precious few deserve the hero badge, and even fewer can bear the burden and temptations that come with the label. That said, how about we just periodically stop spinning, recognize, and celebrate people of integrity, everywhere. Not the fictitious Armstrong brothers and their lookalikes, but the genuine gems. Those good folks who live, love, play, and work with us, every day.

In a world of situational ethics (morality of convenience), it's refreshing and reassuring to know that there are people— lots and lots of good folks—out there who are willing to take great risks, forgo riches, and commit themselves to causes bigger than themselves.

US Anti-Doping Agency CEO, Travis Tygart, under threat of personal harm, is one of the good guys. His mission is to protect clean athletes by exposing those, like Armstrong, who cheat. Jeff Fager, Chairman, CBS News, also joins the club. He, admittedly, helped create the Armstrong myth; however, he and his producer, Michael Raduzky, also relentlessly stayed with the story and reported the myth as it began to unravel. As with Tygart, Raduzky reported on *60 Minutes* that the Armstrong camp personally threatened him.

Another person who was threatened, disparaged, as well as economically harmed by Armstrong is Betsy Andreu, wife of Frankie, Lance Armstrong's former cycling teammate. Her crime: She testified in a lawsuit that she and her husband heard Armstrong tell a doctor in the mid-1990s that he had used an array of performance enhancers. Frankie, she reports, was pushed off the Armstrong team, essentially ending his professional cycling career, for failing to fully step up to the recommended doping program.

Yes! Yes! Yes! We want and need really good people. Take a bow Travis Tygart, take a bow Jeff Fager, take a bow Michael Raduzky, take a bow Betsy Andreu! You've all earned it.

It's Not About the Bike...

There is another good guy, really good guy, and dear friend for over fifteen years, that I would ask to step forward, be recognized, and take a bow. He is Doug Ulman, President and CEO of Livestrong. But asking Doug to take a bow would be a useless request. Doug would—nicely, politely, self-deprecatingly—smile, look away, shrug his shoulders, defer to the entire organization, and scoff at the suggestion. I know he would. That's who he is.

So, as I look closely at the poster that is now in storage with old bed frames, partially completed projects, and random junk, I am reminded of that day long ago in Austin, and I think about what this all means today.

That day was a dynamic celebration of hope, determination, inspiration, and common cause. It was about surviving and thriving with, during, and beyond your cancer diagnosis, or the diagnosis of a loved one. It was about collective caring, unity of spirit, and the power of the possible. It was about tears, laughter, hugs, and goodwill. It was about the visceral knowledge that life is lived in moments, not years.

Yes, Lance and his journey symbolized the theme and galvanized the crowd, but it wasn't and isn't about the bike. On that score, he got it right, he told the truth.

Reflection 39

GLACIER AS LIFE

6:30 a.m.
August 13, 2000
South Davidson Glacier
Alaska
United States of America
Continent of North America
Western Hemisphere
Earth
Solar System
Universe
The Mind of God

A RHYTHMIC CRUNCHING AND PADDING SOUND COMING from just inches above my head breaks the cold, damp stillness. In that foggy place where you try to capture the fleeting echoes of sleep, the sound is both comforting and confusing. Dig—scoop—pour—pad, dig—scoop—pour—pad, dig—scoop—pour—pad, dig—scoop—pour—pad. What the—?

Then I remember what Darsie told us yesterday when we set up camp: Keep the tent posts covered in fresh snow so they won't come loose and pull out. A Good Samaritan with a shovel was the answer to my early-morning question.

Darsie, Bill, and Chris are guides from the Haines-based Alaska Mountain Guides and Climbing School, into whose hands my son Derek and I will entrust our health and safety for the next four days. Seven other mountaineers-in-training, ranging in age from early twenties to midfifties, will do the same.

Darsie, an environmental science graduate from Western Washington University, looks more like an accountant than a guide with fifteen years of mountain experience. He is the cofounder of the school and is clearly competent and in control. Bill studied zoology at the University of Washington and conveys an equal sense of confidence and knowledge. Chris is a rugged ten-year veteran of the Marines who dropped out of flight school and left the military service when he realized that training to kill was not how he wished to move forward with life. All three are friendly, confident guys in their late twenties and early thirties.

"Hot drinks in ten minutes!" yells Bill from the kitchen, a spot we hollowed out of the snow when we first arrived at the south end of the Davidson Glacier. This call for hot drinks is the signal to throw on our boots, gaiters, extra layers of fleece, Gore-Tex jackets, pants, hats, and gloves. Then we unzip the flaps to the vestibule and the outer opening of our two-man tent and walk out onto the prehistoric block of ice and snow.

And so our summer day begins.

Before we get to our hot chocolate, we pass four other tents that look just like ours: multicolored bumps on a pure white background. The first tent houses James, an art dealer and Good Samaritan from North Carolina; Richard, a computer consultant from Australia; and Duane, a dairy farmer, and sled-dog breeder from Wisconsin. The next tent is shared by Avi, a computer consultant from South Africa; Derek, a riverboat pilot from Juneau; and Mosby, an English teacher heading to an American school in Switzerland.

Next is Penn's tent; Penn is a physician from the United Kingdom and our group's only female mountaineer. The guides' tent, a snow lounge, and the kitchen make up the remaining structures in our little community. Of course, we also have a snow latrine complete with a privacy wall, and a distant pee wand that reminds us to limit our areas of contamination.

After a quick breakfast of cold cereal and hot English muffins, we return to our tents, pick up our ice axes, drink more water (hydration is critical in the mountains), smear on plenty of sunscreen and lip protection, and put on our protective helmets. Then, formed up into three four-person rope teams, we head for the slope behind us to practice self-arrest techniques. These exercises consist of learning what to do in case you lose your balance and begin to fall down an icy mountain.

For about two hours, we practice falling on our backs, bellies, and butts as we learn to stop the fall by jabbing our axes into the slope. The guides make the time enjoyable as well as instructive, but this is clearly serious business. Failure to instinctively stab the ice after a sudden fall could result in serious injury or death.

The time on the slope is interesting, fun (especially watching my manchild sliding down the hill—not unlike when he was a little boy), and also fatiguing. Since the cancer diagnosis, surgery, and the beginning of hormone therapy, I have extended periods of strength and stamina, but also daily bouts of body-slamming exhaustion. A quick time-out of twenty minutes or so is all I usually need to bounce back, but I can't always predict when the irresistible urge to lie down will hit me. Sometimes I forget that I am still a cancer patient. Later that afternoon, I will be reminded.

11:30 a.m.

More hot drinks and a lecture on crevasse rescue techniques follow a quick lunch of chicken soup and peanut butter and jelly sandwiches. The Davidson Glacier is crisscrossed with fissures from a few inches to several feet wide—and deeper than most of us care to contemplate. In some, the echo of a falling object never reaches the surface. Our experienced guides know what to look for, but that in no way guarantees that we will not fall or be pulled into an abyss. We pay close attention.

Once formed into our rope teams, we head out toward the single most beautiful view I have ever seen. The mountains towering above, the heavenly cloudscape below, and the pure white virginal canvas stretching before us set a majestic, surreal scene that cannot be described—only experienced. Add in fresh, sweet air that you can taste, and congenial companions, and the stage is set for an extraordinary day.

We walk single file out of camp and head for the long pristine valley and the beckoning white slopes that gradually expose the jagged black peaks of the Fairweather Range. Standing guard is the regal silhouette of Mount Fairweather, rising 15,300 feet into the deep, dark blue Alaskan sky.

For the next two hours, only the sounds of boots breaking snow, hopelessly inadequate cameras clicking, and childlike expressions of awe break the silence of the glacier. The view always changes; the wind whips snow and clouds; and the sun dances with shadows. I can't decide which is more beautiful: the view or the reflection of that light in my son's eyes. On second thought, yes, I can.

As we approach our first peak, the slope gets progressively steeper, and we have to zigzag upward. Physically, this requires that I shift my focus from the scene around me to the footprint trail in front of me. In spite of my months of training and a lean diet that has trimmed me by more than thirty pounds, the buoyancy fueled by adrenaline, inspiration, and beauty is giving way to muscle fatigue and that all-too-familiar urge to simply lie down and rest. At home, this would mean moving twenty yards from my study to the bedroom. But I am not on Village Road in Saline, Michigan—I am on the Davidson Glacier in Southeast Alaska. Rest, at this moment, is not an option—at least not to the primordial ancestor that pushes (harasses) me to continue and not complain.

Fortunately, my cardiovascular system is healthy enough to deal with the altitude and exertion. The lungs that I abused with tobacco from age fifteen to thirty have recovered significantly over the past twenty-two smoke-free years. Years of studying meditation and deep-breathing techniques enable me to shift my focus from the growing muscle pain and fatigue to the task at hand: slogging, step by slow, painful step, closer and closer to the top. I watch the rope that connects me to Penn, and as it moves, so do I. For several minutes, the universe becomes the snakelike crawling of a 10-millimeter rope.

Then the snake stops. I look up; the team ahead of us has reached the peak. I take a deep breath, wipe the sweat off my face, and smile. I've made it!

With renewed strength, I unclip my harness from the team rope and begin the small rock-climb to the top ledge. The rock is very loose; it crumbles beneath my feet. Now is not the time for carelessness. I slow down, find my footing, and climb to meet Derek, who has already sprinted to the top as nimble as a mountain goat. As I take that last step, I remember my pledge to honor those cancer survivors who have inspired me to make this trip, and I say a short prayer of thanks. And, oh yes, my dad and I have a wonderful chat. The tears are cold as the wind strikes my face, but my smile and heart are oh so warm.

4:15 p.m.

After a nice long rest, lots of water, and more sunscreen, we are ready to move on to another peak. I am now confident that I have the strength to go all day. I am also a fool in need of advanced lessons in humility and the virtue of accepting the help of others. I will soon receive both lessons.

The others in my rope party are fine, but for me the way down the slope is more like a controlled fall then a smooth descent. The idea is to lead with the heel of your boot as you build a downward rhythm. To help stabilize each step, it's often easier to break new snow than to follow in someone else's tracks. Of course, you are also keenly aware that the beaten path has passed the no-crevasse-here test and that breaking fresh trail runs a particular risk. I need to preserve as much strength as possible, so I accept the small risk and make new boot prints.

There are two teams in front of ours, and I am the third member on our rope so I can see all but one member of the entire group. Their descent is smooth and measured. They appear to be gliding effortlessly down to the valley. I, on the other hand, am running down the slope to keep the rope between Penn and me from becoming a clothesline. There is no grace in my step, no rhythm; this is work. My quadriceps burn with each clumsy plunge. When we reach the bottom and begin our flat traverse of the valley, Penn hollers back, "Are you all right, love?" I smile and lie as I tap my helmet to signal that all is well.

More water, more sunscreen, more pictures. We trek across the valley floor toward the next peak. Hey, I'm fine! No need for rest. There is no need to ask Chris, our rope guide, to slow down the pace. I can keep up with anybody. Look at me, I'm a mountaineer.

Then, after about an hour, we begin the second ascent of the afternoon.

I make the mistake of focusing on how steeply we must climb to get to the top. For an experienced mountaineer, this is a small incline, but what I see is Mount Everest. I stop seeing the beauty of the glacier; I fixate on every step and the way the rope is moving. Several times I feel my legs starting to buckle—they are screaming for a rest—but instead of listening to my body, I respond by increasing my spot-focus meditation and denying my pain.

Again and again, Penn feels the tug of fatigue on the rope and hollers back, "Are you all right, love? Do you need to rest?"

And each time, the idiot inside me reaches up and taps my helmet. I refuse to hold the team up, to call attention to myself, to admit that I need help. I think of all the cancer survivors and the pain that so many of them have to endure. In comparison, this is just a single gnat in paradise. I hear the words drilled into the head of every boy raised in the 1950s: No pain, no gain. Tough it out. Quit your complaining. Don't be a sissy. And, of course, I remember the words of Sister Mary Ada who told us to offer our suffering up to the poor souls in Purgatory. I smile at the thought and figure that I must be flooding the gates of heaven with newly purified souls, ready for entry.

When the snake pauses for more than a few seconds, I realize that the first team has reached the summit and that soon I will be able to rest. When it's my turn to come on up, I take off my harness and collapse in the snow. The others continue the short rock-climb to the view of the other side, but I do not move, cannot move, will not move. I hear their excitement at the vista spread out before them; I hear them urging me to come see. But I don't care. I do not move, cannot move, will not move. Beauty is for later. Now, I need to rest, lick my wounds, and feel sorry for myself. I will be okay. But for now—I do not move, cannot move, will not move.

Chris is concerned. He stays behind to talk with me. We talk about the cancer treatment; how great it is that I get to do this with one of my sons; his time in the military; the challenges of the mountain. We also talk (or, rather, he talks, and I listen) about the importance of letting him know exactly how I am doing. We can slow down and take breaks whenever I need. The important thing is that I let him know. I can handle the physical challenge, he says, as long as I am honest about how I am feeling.

Chris is compassionate without being patronizing, and it is greatly appreciated. So is the break. I am now ready to climb the last few yards and see what's on the other side.

As I reach the top and look out over the tops of clouds toward the Cathedral Peaks, my pain and fatigue melt away. Visibility is infinite, and the view is like nothing I have ever seen before. I'm standing on the edge of the world, feeling awe, wonder, gratitude, and, most of all, an indescribable spiritual awareness. What a gift this is! I must treasure and respect the offering. I know, too, that this gift is not mine alone. I am accepting it on behalf of all who would be here if they could. Without their energy and inspiration, I would not have made this trip; I would not have climbed this mountain peak; I would not have gained this moment.

Darsie is telling us to put on our harnesses and packs; it is time to climb down and return to base camp. I do not move, cannot move, will not move. But of course I must—and, with hesitation, I do.

7:45 p.m.

This descent is no more graceful than the last, but there is a difference. When we reach the floor of the valley, Penn needs to stop to remove a layer of fleece. Chris asks me if the pace is okay or should he slow it down. I begin to raise my hand to pat my helmet, but I stop halfway and say: "Please slow it down just a bit." I am learning.

Assuming ideal conditions, the journey back to camp will take about two hours. After about an hour, intense fatigue sets in once more and my steps are mixed with stumbles. It is a slow march across the floor of the glacier, the crunch of the snow serving as a metronome. At one point, I look up and see that we are about to descend into a cloud.

To this inexperienced mountain climber from the lower forty-eight, it triggers only appreciation of the spectacular view. To a guide, it means something else—the prospect of a total whiteout, a combination of sun, mist, and snow that all but obliterates visibility. In the late afternoon on a glacier with dangerous crevasses and a tired team of new climbers, this is a grave situation. We will need the keenest instincts and skills of our guides to avoid getting lost and stranded.

Penn, who is only forty feet in front of me, begins to fade into the mist. Chris has already disappeared. The scene is dreamlike, surreal, and—in my happy ignorance—simply beautiful. At one point, the sun is a perfect circle of light piercing the thick mist. The result is the opposite of a shadow: instead of shade in a field of sunshine, there is a small pool of light shining on the snow, like a flashlight piercing the night. I feel the way I did when I was a child in church. I can sense a presence that is both comforting and frightening—not in a scary way, but in the knowledge of its awesome power and force. I have never felt more vulnerable and, strangely, neither have I ever felt more safe.

The irony of my sense of security soon becomes apparent. We reach the next crest to find the other two rope teams formed in a circle. The whiteout has made further travel impossible. We are amid crevasses. We are lost.

I find Derek, who is a little tired, like everyone else, but okay. The three guides huddle; the rest of us stand and speculate. There is a real possibility that we will have to tighten the circle and wait until the storm has cleared, even if it takes all night.

Still, I feel safe. I have not a clue which way to go, but it seems everyone else does. Fortunately, one of these is Chris.

214

His training as a guide and his experience as a Marine help him locate our outbound tracks. Soon, we are lined up in single file heading, once again, into the mist. Duane from Wisconsin feels we are going away from camp, but my money is on Chris.

10:00 p.m.

After a long fifteen minutes, I hear relieved voices and see the beginnings of shadows of small bumps on a pure white background. We're back! By the time we reach camp and collapse in the snow beside our tents, I hear the glorious sound of Bill's voice shouting, "Hot drinks in ten minutes!"

Then I hear my voice: "Thanks, God, it's been quite a summer's day."

Time to Wake Up:
Discover Your Passion and Purpose

CAUTION

THIS JOURNEY IS NOT TO BE TAKEN LIGHTLY. AWAKENING brings acute awareness, accountability, and a profound understanding of choice. No longer will you readily assume the role of victim when confronted with obstacles, disruption, and hardship. Nor will you routinely subjugate your joy and passion to the interests of others. You will instead own and be responsible for the moments of your life, all of them. Clarity lifts the gauze that both protects and restricts what you see and feel.

We now move from the philosophical to the practical. Here's where we will answer the following five questions:

1.   What Is My Mission in Life, What Do I *Choose* to Advance?

2.   How Do I Currently *Choose* to Advance My Healthy Happiness?

3.   If Life Gave Me a Do-Over, What Would I *Choose* to Do Over? What Do I *Choose* to Do Moving Forward?

4.   Once I *Choose* a Goal, How Probable Is Achievement?

5.   How Do I Validate and Support the Healthy Living Goals That I *Choose*?

What Is My Mission in Life, What Do I Choose *to Advance?*

Age-old question, Why was I born? What is my purpose?

Let's begin by developing a first draft of a personal mission statement. Don't worry about the fine-tuning. For now, just write what comes to mind. To help you get started, here's an example:

My personal mission—my life goal—is to progressively and consistently achieve measurably higher levels of physical, emotional, intellectual, economic, and spiritual awareness. I will do this by living a life of integrity, curiosity, authenticity, compassion, happiness, and dedication to the collective needs of all beings. And by assisting others in doing likewise.

A bit lofty, perhaps, but a personal mission statement should reflect an ideal that you aspire to, something grand, an oath proudly pledged! It needs to be easy to recall, subjectively as well as objectively measurable, and organic to the point that it is forever evolving.

Another example:

My personal mission is to be a constant and continuous positive role model for my children and grandchildren. I will demonstrate this by my acts, my deeds, and—most important—my intentions.

Your Turn: Before continuing, write a personal mission statement. Without one, the rest of this book has no context, no personal texture. You are merely yawning in the face of morning light. You will not awaken.

My personal mission is to…

After writing your personal mission statement, ask yourself: What did I expect? What did I discover?

How Do I Currently Choose to Advance My Healthy Happiness?

The most important thing is not life but the good life. The good life, the beautiful life, and the just life are the same.

—Socrates

Remember our definitions

Wellness: wellness is a dynamic objective and subjective progression toward a state of complete physical, intellectual, emotional, spiritual, and social well-being, and not merely the absence of disease or infirmity. Incremental improvements can occur from preconception up to and including a person's last breath.

Thrival: a steady state of achieving higher levels of physical, emotional, intellectual, social, and spiritual awareness by living a life of integrity, curiosity, authenticity, compassion, and dedication to the collective needs of all beings.

At the moment they occur, all actions are motivated by self-interest—not to be confused with selfish, which is the wanton disregard for the interests and well-being of others. We are either running from pain or moving toward pleasure, often a blend of both. Decisions are made and actions are taken in the context of known and available options that we believe will address our immediate needs. There is a perceived subjective payoff. This perception is not necessarily good or bad; it simply is. The educator's (parent, teacher, government, healthcare provider) responsibility/opportunity is to provide awareness, clarity, and expanded options. Once presented—and obstacles removed—the informed individual's responsibility/opportunity is to choose wisely.

Research shows that healthy happiness requires time spent in all six of the dimensions that comprise the art of living.

The six dimensions of the art of living

- Physical (nutrition, sleep, exercise)

- Intellectual stimulation

- Emotional health, happiness, and positive psychology

- Spiritual engagement and mind/body development

- Social interaction

- Economics and personal finance

Physical (nutrition, sleep, exercise). Health professionals can objectively present the newest USDA food guidelines, introduce you to the five food groups, and explain the difference between healthy and unhealthy oils. However, they can't dictate your subjective preference for preparation, presentation, taste, and texture. They can tell you to eat dark green vegetables, but you have to decide if you like broccoli, romaine lettuce, kale, or raw baby spinach.

They can also objectively point out the importance of following exercise guidelines from the American College of Sports Medicine and the American Heart Association. However, you and your doctor have to decide if it will be moderate for thirty minutes a day for five days a week, or vigorous for twenty minutes a day for three days a week. And while an educator can show you a whole host of strength-training exercises, you will have to decide which exercises you enjoy enough to do eight to twelve repetitions, twice a week.

Intellectual stimulation. A health educator can objectively explain the new findings regarding neuroplasticity and show you the brain use-it-or-lose-it research. However, you have to select activities that not only stimulate your brain but that you also enjoy. Playing chess may fire up neurons, but it may also drive you crazy. Is it Mozart? How about the classics or a good graphic novel? Learning a language will do the trick at any age, but so will learning to play a new musical instrument. So, what language? What instrument? How about crossword puzzles and Sudoku?

Professionals can tell you to stay engaged and keep learning new things. However, only you can make the subjective choices that will keep it fun and nurture a beginner's mind until your dying day.

Emotional health, happiness, and positive psychology. A health educator can objectively guide you to research while touting the importance of nurturing your emotional health and the importance of striving to be happy (make that happier). Tal Ben-Shahar from Harvard, Martin Seligman, author of *Authentic Happiness,* and the Dalai Lama are among the many who will show you the evidence and present logical arguments that support positive psychology.

The experts and the literature can explain the whys and the hows. However, you have to search for, identify, and protect what aids your emotional health and makes you happy. By the way, the more joyous you are, the more joyous the people around you become.

Is it time with your pet? How about time with kids and family? Maybe—for you—emotional health is buoyed whenever you complete your daily To Do list or spend time outside playing in the sun. You know what brings you healthy happiness (oh, yes you do) so plan time each day to do it.

Spiritual engagement and mind/body development. A health educator can tell you that spiritual growth brings context to life; that it gives meaning to your every thought and action. Regardless of where you find it—bricks and mortar, open fields, tops of mountains, desert canyons, ocean waves, or cuddled inside a child's laugh—spiritual essence is all around us. As the poem states, "*Spirituality* is forever present without the need of definition, invisible to some, blindingly radiant to others, existing without beckon; eternally ours."

Christ, Moses, Buddha, Mohammad, Lao Tzu, Gandhi, Mother Teresa, Elmo, Winnie, and Piglet too remind us of the importance of finding and following our path to happiness and freedom. However, where is your path? How do you know when you are traveling the right road? Where does it lead today? Where will it take you tomorrow? Tough questions. Once again, only an awakened you will know what actions, activities, people, places, thoughts, and dreams bring peace to your spirit and strength to your body.

Social interaction. A health educator can tell you that John Donne nailed it when he wrote, "No man is an Island, entire of itself; every man is a piece of the Continent, a part of the main; if a clod be washed away by the sea, Europe is the less, as well as if a promontory were, as well as if a manor of thy friends or of thine own were; any man's death diminishes me, because I am involved in Mankind; And therefore never send to know for whom the bell tolls; It tolls for thee."

Though written in the early seventeenth century, the sentiment and fact remain faithful. We need each other for our safety, economic growth, advancement of science and art, and for our emotional and physical well-being.

Health educators can show you objective data all day long that points to the importance of staying connected with others. However, they can't tell you what form of human contact is best for you! Join a square dancing club? How about a bowling league, book club, movie club, church choir, or a softball team? Maybe you're quiet and shy and would prefer to stay somewhat anonymous, so how about e-mail, a chat forum for your favorite hobby, or a social network like Facebook?

Economics and personal finances. A health educator can tell you that a failing economy and poor personal financial management is a huge source of illness-causing stress. But you have to know your personal danger signals and take timely prevention measures. A financial advisor can tell you about the hazards of a balloon mortgage and the risks of escalating interest rates on credit cards. Yet you have to assume responsibility for risky investments, irresponsible spending, and payment defaults.

Here are possible elements and activities:

Physical	Intellectual	Emotional	Spiritual	Social	Economic
Biking	Books	Time with Family	Nature	Time with Family	Paying Bills on Time
Swimming	Puzzles	Hobby Time	Formal Religion	Going to Public Functions	Sticking to a Budget
Jogging	Discussions	Completing To Do Lists	Pets	Time with Colleagues	Review and Cancel Auto Payments for Products and Services Not Used
Team Sports	Staying Current	Meditation	Travel	Texting or Talking with Friends	Brown Bag Lunches
Walking	Chess	TV, Movies, Plays	Scuba Diving	Team Sports	Alcohol in Moderation or Not at All
Healthy Eating	Bridge	Fine Dining	Walks in the Woods		Zero Balance Credit Cards
Adequate Sleep	New Language	Sound Financial Management	Time with Grandchildren		
Strength Training	Music	Music			
Stretching		Heart-to-Heart Talks			
Yoga		Initiating/ Sustaining Meaningful Change			
Martial Arts					

Keep in mind the fact that one element may fit into several sectors. For example—for many individuals—exercise scores in many sectors. A sunrise/sunset bike ride may trigger spiritual satisfaction; walking with your family may earn social, emotional, and physical marks. Swimming laps and light jogging is known to stimulate the release of nitric oxide–triggering eureka moments that lead to problem-solving (intellectual). Playing Frisbee in the park with your dog may fit into physical, emotional, spiritual, and social. You get the point. It's up to you!

Your Turn: Referring to the definitions and examples in this section, write down the current physical, intellectual, emotional, spiritual, social, and economic ways you choose to advance your healthy happiness.

After completing your lists, ask yourself: What did I expect? What did I discover?

If Life Gave Me a Do-Over, What Would I Choose to Do Over? What Do I Choose to Do Moving Forward?

Of course, you know what moves you, what lifts your spirit and shakes your bones. You've always known. Problem is that a lifetime of listening to others, quieting your inner voice, tempering desire with compliance and compromise, and applying a thin, comforting façade of Someday has buried your passion under a confusing jungle of noise, shadows, blur, and distortion.

Spend some time with the following poem. The first part reflects our lack of self-confidence and our dependence upon everyone else to know what is best for us. Our inner voice, our spirit, pleads to be heard but, like speaking to a child, we shush the voice so that the adults can be heard. In the second half of the poem, we have learned to pay attention to our gut, to our heart, and to our instincts. We appreciate the concern of others but focus on personal accountability and self-direction.

Be Very Quiet & Listen...

My ears accept your words but that's where they seem to remain
The vibrations are clear and, yet, distant—
yes, there is logic and the gift is truly appreciated
However, a persistent nudge tugs at my sleeve and
distracts me from the moment

Be still, I say, there are others talking and you must be quiet & listen

I pay attention; I really do, however,
I only catch a spark and then it's gone
What did you say? I heard you speak but I can't seem to follow
A muffled breeze tugs at my sleeve and distracts me from the moment

**Be still, I implore, let those who know—
speak their truth—you must be quiet & listen**

I nod my head; follow directions, and give thanks
for such strong support
Often the direction takes me to a place
where I feel safe but somehow not secure
An echo of a whisper tugs at my sleeve and
distracts me from the moment

Be still, I shout, who are you to contradict—
you must be quiet & listen!

The companion voice wishes to speak but is smothered
by noise from the street and
Daunted by scolding doubts from within…

Years, reflections, and nurturing wisdom bring clarity to the voices
I listen with all my senses and pay close attention
to the whispers particularly those of
A used-to-be-nudge that tugs at my sleeve and
distracts me from the moment

Speak up, I say, and I will be quiet and I will listen

I pay attention as I strain to hear the pleas and
questions hidden among the words
What did you say? Sometimes, my ability to understand
is impaired by the noise of emotion
The goddess tugs at my sleeve bringing both a
cleansing breeze and a basket of dreams

Speak up, I implore, and reveal the truth—
I will be quiet and I will listen

I nod my head, follow directions, and give thanks
for such strong support
Often the direction takes me to a place where
I may not always feel safe but I do feel secure
A clear voice tugs at my sleeve and protects me from distractions

**Speak up, I shout, keep me aware of contradictions—
I will be quiet and I will listen**

The companion voice speaks freely high above
the noise of the street and is
Encouraged by a growing confidence that glows from within

Your Turn:

1. Write down three risks you've considered taking but have been stopped by the YeahBut syndrome.

2. Write your obituary (assume you die today, sorry). At a minimum, write down achievements and at least one other item in shown in **bold**:

    - Name (including nickname, if any):
    - Age at death:
    - Place of birth:
    - Name of parents:
    - Childhood (siblings, stories, schools, friends):
    - Marriage(s) (date of, place, name of spouse):
    - Children (names and current residence):
    - Education (high school, college, university, other):
    - Designations, awards, and other recognitions:
    - Employment:
    - **Hobbies, sports, interests, activities:**
    - Charitable, religious, political and other affiliations:
    - **Achievements:**
    - **Disappointments:**
    - Unusual attributes, humor, other stories:
    - A published quote that sums up your life:
    - **Six words to sum up your life:**

3. Great news! You get to live another ten years. Edit the obituary accordingly.

4. Make a list of the books you've read over the past five years.

5. Ask your best friend where your passion lies (really helpful).

6. What magazines do you read?

7. Favorite websites?

8. What kinds of movies do you like?

9. Reflect on the above and journal your thoughts for three days (fifteen minutes, first thing in the morning, within an hour of waking).

10. Go back and reread your two obituaries.

Okay, reflect on the ten points: What would you do over? Nothing? That's okay. The bigger question is, what do you commit to doing moving forward?

After writing down the answers to the two previous questions, ask yourself: What did I expect? What did I discover?

Once I Choose *a Goal, How Probable Is Achievement?*

Indeed, thoughts are the gateway to action. If you believe something strongly enough and that something is within the realm of possibility, you will do everything you possibly can to make it so. Self-fulfilling prophecy applies to both success and failure.

Possibility is a fact and is governed by physical laws. Probability is statistical and subjective and governed by preparation, passion, and spirit. Beyond the physical laws, if you believe you can, you can. If you believe you can't, you can't. If you believe you will, you will. If you believe you won't, you won't. You are the author, producer, and director of your actions. You control the script. You are the one who says, "Action!" You are the one who says, "Cut!"

Without passion, setting long-term goals is meaningless regardless of available resources. In most cases, strong passion will trump low opportunity.

Using the Probability Guide, select one of your achievement goals and chart both the passion you feel toward the goal, as well as your available resources (opportunity). The point of intersection will give you an idea of how viable this goal is.

Measuring Passion—Factors to Consider

- Day/night dreams
- Journal notes
- Obituary-writing exercise
- Belief in ability to achieve

Probability Guide

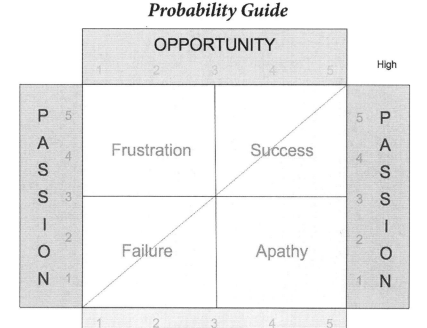

copyright, mh samuelson, 2015

- Fear factor

- Possible short-term and long-term consequences

- Topics of conversation

- Reading list

- Risks stopped by the YeahBut…

- Animation and affect when thinking about or discussing with a friend

- Facial expressions

- Gesturing and gesticulation

- Voice volume, inflection, and intonation

- Eyes widening and pupil dilation
- Heart rate
- Galvanic skin response (sweat)

Measuring Opportunity—Realities to Consider

- Physical ability
- Finances
- Intellectual capacity
- Personal history
- Impact on others
- Responsibilities (family, pets, social, job, for examples)

After using the Probability Guide, ask yourself: What did I expect? What did I discover?

How Do I Validate and Support the Healthy Living Goals That I Choose?

> *Everybody wants to have a goal: I gotta get to that goal, I gotta get to that goal, I gotta get to that goal. Then you get to that goal, and then you gotta get to another goal. But in between goals is a thing called life that has to be mindfully lived and enjoyed—and if you don't, you're a fool.*
>
> —Sid Caesar

Change! No matter how badly we want it for ourselves or for others, sustainable, meaningful change is a process, not an event. The process is linear and sequential. It progresses from intellectual, to emotional, to visceral before it becomes cellular.

- The Intellectual Phase: We are informed (passive)

- The Emotional Phase: We are engaged (active)

- The Visceral Phase: We are moved to action (active)

- The Cellular Phase: We are the change (passive)

Writing down and announcing goals like losing weight, quitting smoking, sobriety, or starting an exercise program makes us feel good, even righteous. Friends applaud, Mom is happy, Oprah smiles; the world is delighted with our decision. In fact, the external shouts of approval often drown out our internal hesitations, fears, doubts, and even desires.

All too often, externally prescribed *shoulds* trump internally driven *wants*. And, while the intellectual I Should thinking may trigger engagement, it's the visceral, bone-shaking, soul-lifting I Want (subjective well-being) motivation that leads to sustained behavior change. The ideal is for desire to trigger behavior that satisfies and advances physical health, spiritual awareness, and emotional need.

To determine whether your healthy living goals are truly yours and not just the urgings of your Aunt Betty, Dr. Phil, or your significant other, you need to monitor whether or not your actions are advancing or hindering your current chosen path. If you are constantly blocking goal attainment, it's time to question your passion, or just maybe you need to restate your goal in terms of what *you* want to do and not merely echo the perceived wishes of others.

At a minimum, for the next fourteen days—within one hour of getting out of bed—write down your goal and the answers to the following questions and notice that it is all about choice—your choice.

1. Reflecting on the past twenty-four hours, what did you choose to do to advance your goal?

    ▪ What was the short-term payoff?

    ▪ If continued, what will be the long-term payoff?

2. Reflecting on the past twenty-four hours, what did you choose to do that sabotaged your goal?

    ▪ What was the short-term payoff?

    ▪ If continued, what will be the long-term consequences?

3. Planning for the next twenty-four hours, what will you choose to do to advance your goal?

    ▪ What will be the short-term payoff?

    ▪ If continued, what will be the long-term payoff?

    ▪ What challenges do you anticipate?

    ▪ What is your mitigation strategy?

After completing this validation task, ask yourself: What did I expect? What did I discover?

CLOSING THOUGHTS: SERIOUSLY, ALFIE, WHAT'S IT ALL ABOUT?

FIFTEEN YEARS HAVE PASSED, AND, OF COURSE, THE SCAR remains. It's always there, the scar; it's always there. I welcome its presence. It, the scar, has taken me to the far reaches of our world and deep into my soul. Without the scar, without the cancer journey, I'm convinced that I would sit with Mr. Mitty, daydreaming about what could be, instead of reflecting on what was and appreciating what is.

I look in the mirror and say to myself, how strange, this ugly package that ushered such beauty into my life, how strange, indeed.

So, Alfie, is it about finding beauty under rocks buried in the mud and muck? Is it about reflections on the past that lead to visions of the future yielding an appreciation for the now? Is it about awakening to the tug of the Divine Thread, holding on tight, hoping that the knot doesn't slip? Is it about reaching out to strangers and discovering that they are my brothers and sisters, that they are, indeed, me? Is it about being okay with being lost in midsentence?

Is it about listening to the silence that follows the echoes? Is it about the eternal layers of texture seemingly just out of our reach? Is it about the shadows? Is it about embracing the pain and letting go? Is it about swapping judgment in favor of compassion? Is it about love and forgiveness in the face of unspeakable horror?

Or is it just for the moment we live?

Yes. Life, I hear Alfie whisper, it is about moving forward with optimism, about running to pick up rocks, digging in the mud with the full expectation of finding treasure. It, life, is about viewing the past as an agnostic teacher—one who never judges but, instead, only records and stores for future consideration. Life is about reaching forward armed with both trepidation and hope, embracing moments with the insatiable curiosity of a young child, a little one, leaping and listening with a beginner's mind.

And, yes, nods Alfie, life is a heartbeat, a sigh, a smile, a hug, a tear, a laugh, a glimpse. Life is a moment of pain, hope, despair, and prayer. Life is a shiver of fear in the dark and a shiver of joy in the light. Life is a shadow of regret and promise as the sun slips down, and a ray of hope and promise as it rises up once again.

ABOUT THE AUTHOR

OVER THE PAST FORTY YEARS—FROM BOSTON TO BRUSSELS, London to Little Rock, Peoria to Paris, and Harrisburg to Havana—Michael Samuelson has lectured on leadership, health promotion, patient experience, health policy, disease prevention, and the dynamics of behavior change.

An author of five books and numerous articles on leadership and behavior change, his work has been featured on the ABC News program *20/20, The CBS Morning Show,* CNN, and MSNBC as well as numerous national print publications including the *New York Times, Boston Globe, The Lancet, Employee Benefit News, American Journal of Health Promotion, Business Week*, and *USA Today.*

Michael completed his graduate studies at the University of Michigan, is a Vietnam-era veteran of the US Air Force (1967– 1971), and a recipient of the Commander's Coin of Excellence from the US Army Center for Health Promotion and Preventive Medicine.

His distinguished professional résumé includes successful entrepreneur, senior executive in the health insurance industry,

CEO, university professor, and US health policy advisor. His writings, audio work, and behavior change programs have been distributed to millions throughout the world and have been publicly endorsed by scientists, politicians, advocacy organizations, business leaders, and media personalities including George H.W. Bush, Betty Ford, C. Everett Koop, Ken Blanchard, Livestrong, and Larry King.

Practicing what he preaches, Michael is an avid world trekker with high-altitude mountain adventures logged in Asia, Europe, Africa, South America, Alaska, and throughout the US lower forty-eight—all after the age of fifty and after diagnosis of and treatment for breast cancer.

Other books by Michael Samuelson

- *Voices from the Edge: Life Lessons from the Cancer Community*

- *What Would Mickey Say: Coaching Men to Health and Happiness*

- *Personal Stress Management: Turning Challenges into Opportunities*

Contact Michael at m.samuelson@mac.com or
www.SamuelsonWellness.com
He would like to hear from you.